Teresa Pica
Associate Director
Educational Linguistics/TESOL

Writing Our Lives:
Reflections on Dialogue Journal
Writing with Adults Learning English

Language in Education
Theory and Practice

Writing Our Lives:
Reflections on Dialogue Journal
Writing with Adults Learning English

Joy Kreeft Peyton and Jana Staton, Eds.

PRENTICE HALL REGENTS Englewood Cliffs, New Jersey 07632

Library of Congress Cataloging-in-Publication Data

Writing our lives: reflections on dialogue journal writing with
   adults learning English / Joy Kreeft Peyton and Jana Staton, editors
  ; prepared by National Clearinghouse on Literacy Education.
     p. cm. — (Language in education ; 77)
   "A publication of CAL, Center for Applied Linguistics."
   Includes bibliographical references.
   ISBN 0-13-969338-6
    1. English language—Study and teaching—Foreign speakers.
  2. Dialogues—Authorship—Study and teaching. 3. Diaries—
Authorship—Study and teaching. 4. Adult education. I. Peyton,
Joy Kreeft. II. Staton, Jana. III. National Clearinghouse on
Literacy Education. IV. Center for Applied Linguistics. V. Series.
PE1128.A2W76 1991
428'.007—dc20   91-6444
                                                 CIP

Language in Education: Theory and Practice 77

This publication was prepared with funding from the
Office of Educational Research and Improvement, U.S.
Department of Education, under contract No. RI
88062010. The opinions expressed in this report do not
necessarily reflect the positions or policies of OERI or
ED.

Editorial/production supervision: Anne Graydon
Interior design: Elizabeth R. Rangel
Cover design: Ben Santora
Pre-press buyer: Ray Keating
Manufacturing buyer: Lori Bulwin

Printed in the United States of America

10 9 8 7 6 5 4 3 2 1

ISBN   0-13-969338-6

Prentice-Hall International (UK) Limited, *London*
Prentice-Hall of Australia Pty. Limited, *Sydney*
Prentice-Hall Canada Inc., *Toronto*
Prentice-Hall Hispanoamericana, S.A., *Mexico*
Prentice-Hall of India Private Limited, *New Delhi*
Prentice-Hall of Japan, Inc., *Tokyo*
Simon & Schuster Asia Pte. Ltd., *Singapore*
Editora Prentice-Hall do Brasil, Ltda., *Rio de Janeiro*

Language in Education:
Theory and Practice

ERIC (Educational Resources Information Center) is a nationwide network of information centers, each responsible for a given educational level or field of study. ERIC is supported by the Office of Educational Research and Improvement of the U.S. Department of Education. The basic objective of ERIC is to make current developments in educational research, instruction, and personnel preparation readily accessible to educators and members of related professions.

The ERIC Clearinghouse on Languages and Linguistics (ERIC/CLL), one of the specialized clearinghouses in the ERIC system, is operated by the Center for Applied Linguistics (CAL). ERIC/CLL is specifically responsible for the collection and dissemination of information on research in languages and linguistics and on the application of research to language teaching and learning.

ERIC/CLL commissions recognized authorities in languages and linguistics to write about current issues in the field. The resultant monographs, intended for use by educators, researchers, and others interested in language education, are published jointly by CAL and Prentice Hall Regents under the series title, *Language in Education: Theory and Practice*. The series includes practical guides for classroom teachers, state-of-the-art papers, research reviews, and collected reports.

Publications in the *Language in Education: Theory and Practice* series can be purchased directly from Prentice Hall Regents. Reproductions are also available from the ERIC Document Reproduction Service, Alexandria, Virginia.

For further information on the ERIC system, ERIC/CLL, and ERIC/CLL publications, write to ERIC Clearinghouse on Languages and Linguistics, Center for Applied Linguistics, 1118 22nd Street, NW, Washington, DC 20037.

Whitney Stewart, Series Editor

National Clearinghouse on Literacy Education
An Adjunct ERIC Clearinghouse

In September 1989, the Center for Applied Linguistics (CAL) was awarded a contract to expand the activities of the ERIC Clearinghouse on Languages and Linguistics (ERIC/CLL) through the establishment of an Adjunct ERIC Clearinghouse, the National Clearinghouse on Literacy Education (NCLE). The specific focus of NCLE is literacy education for limited-English proficient adults and out-of-school youth.

The creation of NCLE enables ERIC/CLL to expand the *Language in Education: Theory and Practice* series to include monographs targeted specifically to literacy educators working with language minority adults and youth. The purpose of the monographs is to help practitioners assist these individuals in achieving full literacy in English, and whenever possible, in their native languages. ERIC/CLL expects to publish two NCLE monographs per year in the LIE series.

Monographs commissioned by NCLE will be written by recognized authorities in adult literacy education and ESL (English as a second language). They will be edited and prepared for publication by NCLE staff members. The editing and production of *Writing Our Lives: Reflections on Dialogue Journal Writing with Adults Learning English* were coordinated by Elizabeth S. Rangel.

For further information on NCLE publications and services, contact the National Clearinghouse on Literacy Education, Center for Applied Linguistics, 1118 22nd Street, NW, Washington, DC 20037.

Elizabeth S. Rangel, NCLE Publications Coordinator

Contents

Acknowledgments

We are grateful to the many practitioners working in adult literacy education who took the time to discuss their work for this volume. Because of their efforts, we have been able to compile the most up-to-date work that we know of on the use of dialogue journals with adults developing literacy. We are also grateful to Elsa Auerbach and Suzanne Irujo for their extremely helpful comments on an earlier manuscript.

Introduction

Creating an Attitude of Dialogue in Adult Literacy Instruction

Jana Staton
Center for Applied Linguistics
Washington, DC

From the earliest days of the Dialogue Journal Project at the Center for Applied Linguistics (CAL), we saw a major role for dialogue journals in adult literacy settings, even though at that time (1980) we knew of no use in that context. Gradually, as our publications and the newsletter *Dialogue* (1982-1989) reached teachers and researchers working in adult literacy education, more and more people affirmed our belief that dialogue journals could meet the need of adult literacy learners for a functional, interactive, self-generated reading and writing experience, particularly when the language involved is the learner's second language.

This book is a straightforward guide to dialogue journal use. The audience includes teachers, tutors, and educators training others: The individual literacy instructor, facing a crowded classroom filled with a symphony of languages; the volunteer tutor, able to spend time with a single student; and educators training teachers and tutors who are deeply committed to making literacy instruction professional and effective. Such teachers and volunteers are working out of a deep commitment to teaching and to the power of literacy.

For each of these audiences, we wanted to create a book that would be practical and useful, and that would address the underlying principles of dialogue journals as well as provide practical methods for effective use. Part I is an overview—what dialogue journals are, what the written interaction involves, some issues that need to be addressed, and some questions often raised by teachers.

In Part II, experienced adult literacy instructors provide close-up descriptions of how they have adapted the dialogue journal practice to meet students' and teachers' goals and needs in a diversity of settings. Parts III and IV focus on using dialogue journals with beginning writers and for training teachers and tutors. To complement this diversity of classroom accounts, Part V provides a comprehensive discussion of the various benefits of dialogue journals for students and teachers.

Origins and Spread of Dialogue Journal Communication

Although dialogue journals are just now becoming more widely used in adult literacy settings, they have been adopted since 1980 in many other educational settings. Our first research project in 1979-1980 described their creation and use by a teacher in Los Angeles, Leslee Reed, with native English speaking students (Staton, Shuy, Peyton, & Reed, 1988). From that project, their use has spread in primary, elementary, middle school, and high school classes for purposes of improving classroom communication and writing competency and developing students' practical reasoning and problem-solving abilities. Dialogue journals are also widely used today in all levels of English-as-a-second-language (ESL) and foreign language instruction, deaf education, and in college and graduate courses, particularly for teacher training (cf. Dialogue Journal Resources, this volume).

Although this book focuses primarily on adults learning to read and write in English as a second language, the principles and practices described are relevant to and can be found in programs for adults becoming literate in their mother tongue as well.

The Role of Dialogue in Learning

Teaching the purely technical aspect of the procedure is not difficult. The difficulty lies rather in the creation of a new attitude, that of dialogue, so absent from our own upbringing and education....Dialogue is an I-Thou relationship, and thus necessarily a relationship between two Subjects.

Paulo Freire, 1973, p. 52

In this introduction, I discuss some of the "whys" for dialogue journal use in adult second language literacy programs, focusing particularly on the power of genuine dialogue as the essential context for all learning. Freire sees the genuine learning situation as an "I-Thou relationship between two Subjects" who are equals with different kinds of knowledge (Freire, 1973, p. 52), as opposed to situations where someone is simply "teaching" regardless of whether any learning happens.

Many adult English classes now provide cooperative social interaction experiences that make school a place of learning for the first time for many students. The dialogic relationship between teacher and students, and among the students as peers, creates a social context in which the strange new language so long possessed only by others becomes a language possessed by and useful for oneself.

For all the success of the new social interaction methods, there is a common theme in recent discussions of adult education. Learning to make meaning out of print and to use the written word effectively turns out to be far more difficult, and far less successful, for the second language learner than does learning spoken English. For example, Pat Rigg's account of the struggle of a 45-year-old woman trying to become literate (Rigg, 1985) pinpoints the great gaps between the complexity of Petra's life, the words on the pages, and the assumptions of her tutors. But, it doesn't have to be this way, as Rigg recognizes and perceptively points out; the gap can be narrowed if teacher/tutor and student can dialogue about common life experiences. The processes that occur in effective oral language learning can occur in reading and writing as well, if reading and writing are understood as fundamentally dialogic.

The popularity of dialogue journals in adult literacy contexts, in fact, grows from this new understanding that all language acquisition is a process of social interaction. Many adult literacy teachers are committed to using social interaction processes in teaching oral English as a second language but have had difficulty finding effective means to make reading and writing acts of mutual social construction. Dialogue journals are one way of making overt, for teachers and for students, the nature of reading and writing as negotiated language interactions, in which meaning is developed over successive turns as both partners question, comment, clarify, evaluate, and elaborate on a topic.

A written dialogue between student and teacher or tutor is thus entirely unlike having students keep journals on their own. The private journal provides practice in writing, but it gives the student no assistance to go beyond what he or she already knows how to do. In contrast, written dialogues with a teacher, a classroom aide, or even with a more advanced student, provide guided assistance to the learner in expressing ideas and feelings, describing and elaborating on experience, and reflecting more and more critically on that experience.

This concept of guided assistance in dialogic learning, growing out of the developmental theories of Vygotsky (1978, 1986), has often been called "interactional scaffolding" (Cazden, 1983). The term is intended to convey the image of the teacher providing the student whatever support or assistance is needed. The result of such embedded assistance is that the learner is enabled to acquire not just the actions or skills being demonstrated, but far more important, the internal "self-talk" that a competent person uses to guide his or her own activity. Adult learners who have had no previous schooling or who have failed in earlier attempts to read and write must acquire a new set of self-guiding instructions about the connections between printed words on a page and their own lived experience. Such self-talk involves the metacognitive strategies that successful readers and writers use to make sense out of print and to connect thoughts with written words. Acquiring such self-guiding cognitive processes will require unlearning a great many counterproductive, inhibiting thoughts: "I can't read this." "Written words are about things I don't know anything about." "The only way to read is to spell out each word."

The dialogue journal interaction creates a context of equality and power symmetry that leads to trust between learner and teacher or tutor.

This condition of trust and mutual engagement paradoxically enables the learner to let go of the adult defenses that impede language acquisition and to become more like the open, unanxious, risk-taking young child. We have long recognized that young children are innately programmed to make mistakes and keep trying at a task; as a result they learn languages and become literate with little effort up to a certain age. Then, their need to be correct, not to make mistakes, gets in the way of openness to learning. The Counseling-Learning approach to second language learning is based on Curran's theory (1976) that the adult needs to re-experience a childlike state of dependency without losing adult ego-strengths. Dialogue journals provide the opportunity for learners to re-enter this childlike state in writing, while keeping their adult status intact in social settings.

The practice of dialogue journal use looks deceptively simple: Give students a booklet and ask them to write something. There is a danger that teachers new to the practice will see only this visible component—the written journal—and overlook the dialogic structure and the crucial relationship with another mind that must develop. Effective dialogue journal use is a system with three equally important components: (1) the written communication itself, (2) the dialogic conversation, and (3) the responsive relationship between a literacy learner and a more competent member of a literate culture.

MODEL OF DIALOGUE JOURNAL COMMUNICATION
Written Form of Communication

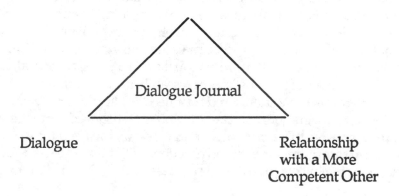

Dialogue

Relationship
with a More
Competent Other

Each component contributes equally to the potentially powerful effect of a written dialogic conversation, as the diagram illustrates.

The Contribution of Dialogue Journals to the Needs of the Adult Literacy Learner

> As an alternative to the banking approaches to second language education, I propose a method in which teachers and adult and adolescent students, even at the earliest levels of language proficiency, begin to find and elaborate their own generative themes and to connect their existential experience to the world of those whose language they are learning. This approach...helps students not only to build critically their own ideas and views about vital issues, but also to build their own words in the new language and to act upon them.
>
> Tomas Graman, 1988, p. 444

Recent studies show that adults begin to drop out of literacy programs after fewer than 50 hours of instruction (Sticht, 1988). While the various reasons for such attrition are still not well understood, there is agreement that too few adults in literacy classes move beyond the mastery of decoding skills to acquire functional literacy—that is, literacy to the level at which the learner can use written language independently for both work and personal needs. For too many adult literacy students, written words remain unconnected to their own experience.

For these students, dialogue journals are one way to provide functional literacy experiences that are personalized, responsive, critical, and reflective. A review of the most recent research and discussions of adult literacy programs has underscored four needs of adult literacy education to which dialogue journals can contribute: (1) the need for materials that are responsive to learners' lives and work; (2) the need for literacy activities that are more complex and functional; (3) the need to transform literacy learning into a more dialogic process; and (4) the need to enable learners to become self-directed and empowered in the classroom setting.

1. Materials need to reflect students' lives.

Auerbach and Burgess (1985), Kazemek (1988), and Sticht (1988), in reviewing the state of adult literacy education, all stress that the materials used in literacy programs continue to be reductive in nature and unrelated to learners' reality. Graman argues that learners need opportunities to connect their classroom tasks to their existential experience, "to build their own words in the new language and to act upon them" (Graman, 1988, p. 444). This must happen at the earliest levels of linguistic proficiency, instead of only at the most advanced.

Allowing students to generate topics of interest for discussion in written form in their dialogue journals, as well as in oral class discussions, provides teachers with opportunities to create individualized reading texts in their responses.

The articles by Janet Isserlis, Laura Klos Sokol, and Loren McGrail in this book demonstrate how the rich, complexly woven content of adult lives—caring for a premature baby, or discussing family, and especially marital, relationships—can be brought into the classroom and embedded in literacy tasks through the use of dialogue journals.

2. Literacy extends beyond basic skills.

Literacy is now recognized as a highly complex cultural phenomenon, one whose meaning is largely determined by the functional uses of literacy in a particular culture. Rather than being a simple set of universal "basic skills" that anyone can learn quickly, literacy is defined as a "relative phenomenon, one that is both personal and social,...it depends on the reader's and writer's purposes and aims for engaging in literacy acts, and it varies according to the nature of the text" (Kazemek, 1988, p. 467). Literacy experiences need to encompass the political and social concerns of students, and should include the complex kinds of tasks that adults must accomplish in their lives, such as negotiating with family members about child care and work schedules, finding new jobs, or coping with immigration processes.

Literacy is no longer defined by literacy educators only in terms of linguistic competencies, even though most adult literacy students probably begin with that traditional definition. For example, Smokey Wilson's chapter describes how her use of tape-recorded dialogues created opportunities for a student to move beyond reading words to reading for meaning. By constructing her own interpretations of books, the student "learned to talk about texts" in a way that connects her reading to her own life in a transformative, meaning-making process.

David Spener demonstrates the great flexibility of an interactive dialogue for constructing appropriately complex tasks for beginning writers, and describes where and why his creative approaches sometimes failed as well as where they succeeded.

3. Literacy is structurally dialogic, not monologic.

Paulo Freire first saw that successful literacy for adult learners requires an I-Thou dialogue where both participants confront each other as knowledgeable equals in a situation of genuine two-way communication. Dialogue journals are just one way that such genuine two-way communication can happen for students and teachers in the literacy classroom. Dialogue journal use can embody the four principles of Freire's dialogic model of adult literacy education (Faigin, 1985): (1) A true dialogue among learners and the teacher is made possible; (2) the learner is treated with respect as a functioning member of society with a contribution to make; (3) the teacher demonstrates that he or she considers the experiences and beliefs of the students to be valid; (4) learning consists of a critical examination of one's reality for the purpose of taking positive action for change.

While many teachers would agree with these philosophical principles, it is difficult to find practical means to realize the principles so that students will grasp them and participate. Dialogue journals can make these abstracted principles very concrete; they can be a genuine instantiation of the Freirean model. Of course, a written dialogue can either be used for true critical reflection on social reality or for mundane, nonreflective communication. But when the writing is at its best, these individual private dialogues create structured opportunities for teacher and student to reflect and re-reflect on social reality, opportunities that are seldom as readily present in the classroom.

The descriptions of dialogue journal use in this volume stress the social, collaborative nature of the dialogic process, and show how dialogue journals can support a reflective, interactive classroom.

4. Adult literacy learners need to become self-directed and empowered.

Among the criticisms of traditional adult literacy education is that students remain passive instead of participating in generating their own themes, bringing issues into the classroom for shared discussion, and learning that the teacher is not all-powerful. However, the reality is that many literacy classes are filled with tired adults, at the end of a long work day, hoping to learn a little without expending much energy, and still expecting the teacher to do the work. A simple, personalized, written dialogue can contribute to the empowering of students as meaning-makers. And an active dialogue helps provide some of the energy and motivation for learning.

Janet Isserlis describes in her chapter in this volume how the dialogue journal partnership fostered her students' independence, so that they eventually arranged for additional student-led class sessions where they took on many of the teacher's facilitating roles. In Part IV, Lenore Balliro and Melody Schneider show how the dialogue journal readily extends to developing confidence and empowerment in teacher and tutor training.

Overview of This Volume

Dialogue journals, like any other kind of human communication, are a context-based practice, useful in the context of an ongoing teacher-student relationship and able to succeed with wide variations. Yet, there are some general rules of thumb that most teachers have found useful. Paul Jones opens the book in Part I with a succinct description of what dialogue journals are, and Joy Peyton discusses the specific issues to be taken into consideration when working with adults, building on the most common comments and questions of adult literacy teachers about dialogue journals. Jack Wigfield raises a number of questions about dialogue journal use for reflective consideration. We have also included a description of dialogue journals in Spanish by Dan Rabideau. Part I provides the broadest possible guidelines for teachers and tutors who want to know how to begin.

As we asked practicing adult educators to contribute to this volume, we encouraged them to include their own questions about and problems with dialogue journal use. We saw these accounts as a rich tapestry inviting comments, questions, comparisons, and reflection. In Part II, Smokey Wilson, Janet Isserlis, Diane Poole, Laura Klos Sokol and Loren McGrail provide close-up descriptions of how they have used dialogue journals to meet students' and teachers' goals in a diversity of settings. In Part III, David Spener and Julietta Davis describe their work with beginning writers, and in Part IV, Lenore Balliro and Melody Schneider report on the use of dialogue journals in the education of literacy teachers and tutors. These different contributions demonstrate the active, creative role of the teacher in making dialogue journals successful.

As a balance to the specific discussions of different uses in practice, Part V is an extended and persuasive discussion by Paul Jones of the benefits of dialogue journals for both students and teachers. Drawing on his own experience as a teacher and on a survey of many other adult second language instructors, Jones provides extensive examples and clarifies the potential benefits. Jones stresses that whatever the specific gains in literacy skills, the basic value of written dialogue is in the development of communication, rapport, and understanding. He points out that dialogue journals may be the only classroom practice that is as deeply rewarding for the teacher as for each student.

Innovations and Next Steps

> Literacy is an ethical endeavor that has as its goal the liberation of people for intelligent, meaningful, and humane action upon the world.
>
> Francis Kazemek, 1988, p. 467

Our view of literacy education agrees with that of Kazemek: We see it as a social and ethical endeavor leading toward greater liberation. This book represents the current state of the art of dialogue journal use with adults learning English. It is our hope that wider knowledge of the power inherent in written dialogic interaction will lead to more innovative uses and to creative solutions to some of the logistical difficulties they pose for the adult literacy instructor. For example, uses of dialogue journals between learners and persons other than the professional teacher are not reflected in this book as common practices. Also, we have not found examples of how dialogue journals could be part of a comprehensive, open-ended program for assessing student progress. Because these seem such logical extensions of dialogue journal use, we briefly discuss these possibilities here.

Literacy helpers as dialogue partners.

One interesting new development that may become more common in the next decade is Kazemek's suggestion (1988) that the collaborative learning circle, or problem-posing circle, include one or two "literacy helpers," recruited from the social-cultural network of the learners, along with the teacher-facilitator. Kazemek sees these literacy helpers as crucial links between the trained teacher and very beginning-level adult students. Such literacy helpers could become the dialogue journal partners for new students. As newly literate guides, they would also benefit from this experience in a continuing literate conversation. The teacher could and should also keep dialogue journals with one or two students in the circle and also with the literacy helpers, but the sheer numerical problem of writing with many students could in this way be solved.

Tutors as dialogue partners.

We thought when we began this volume that one of the major practical uses of dialogue journals would be in the tutorial relationship that occurs in many adult literacy programs. But, during the year we solicited articles, no one in the field was able to describe this use, although Melody Schneider describes the use of dialogue journals for training tutors in her article. The value of the tutor in literacy development lies in the personal relationship and attention that the tutor can provide; a written dialogue would allow the tutor and tutee together to construct a literate text about their interests that could serve as the basis for discussion and further reading.

One practical constraint on dialogue journal use in the tutorial setting is that tutors and tutees typically meet only once a week, and have no means of exchanging a dialogue journal directly except during the session. However, in teacher training programs that meet only once a week, we have found it effective to mail a journal back and forth between sessions. The students write during class time and give the journals to the instructor, who responds and mails them back the next day. It seems that a similar process could be followed in tutorial partnerships as well.

In smaller communities, there may be other creative ways to solve the logistical problems of exchanging the journal so that it supplements but does not dominate the tutorial session.

Holistic assessment of learners' progress.

The adult literacy field has become increasingly interested in means of assessing learners' progress in qualitative ways. Particularly in programs that adopt a whole language, learner-centered approach to literacy as a complex activity, there is a need for methods that are consistent with these underlying pedagogical principles. The value of using dialogue journals for evaluating progress is twofold: For teachers, the dialogues provide unassisted, unedited samples of student writing and reading comprehension as students become more and more able to read and respond fluently to the teacher's entries. For students, journals provide a highly visible, convincing demonstration that they can write the way a literate adult writes. Many adult literacy students have great difficulty believing that they are making substantial progress. Being able to look back through regular entries over several months is an excellent way to provide them with evidence that they are acquiring real competency.

An Attitude of Dialogue

Dialogue journals reflect a perspective on language, literacy, and learning that is radically different from, even opposed to, traditional didactic teaching described by Freire (1973) as the banking concept. Dialogue journals fall within a Freirean, whole language, constructivist philosophy, with the virtue of not requiring any particular intensive training or in-depth knowledge of Freire, Vygotsky, or other educational theorists. But, they do require a certain attitude, or set of beliefs, in order to work. In particular, success in using dialogue journals seems to require from teachers a low need to control their students' actions and a high need to find out and use their students' knowledge and experiences for learning—what Freire calls an "attitude of dialogue."

In other words, adult literacy educators considering using dialogue journals need to reflect on their willingness to allow their students to take more responsibility for their own learning, and on their belief in their students' knowledge and experience as the foundation for acquiring literacy.

References

Auerbach, E.R. & Burgess, D. (1985). The hidden curriculum of survival ESL. *TESOL Quarterly, 19*(3), 475-495.

Cazden, C.B. (1983). Adult assistance to language development: Scaffolds, models and direct instruction. In R. Parker & F. Davis (Eds.), *Developing literacy: Young children's use of language* (pp. 3-18). Newark, DE: International Reading Association.

Curran, C. (1976). *Counseling-learning in second languages.* Apple River, IL: Apple River Press.

Dialogue, The Newsletter About Dialogue Journals. Collected Issues, Vol.I-VI, 1982-89. Washington, DC: Center for Applied Linguistics.

Faigin, S. (1985). *Basic ESL literacy from a Freirean perspective: A curriculum unit for farmworker education.* Essay for the degree of Master of Education, University of British Columbia. (ERIC Document Reproduction Service No. ED 274 196)

Freire, P. (1973). *Education for critical consciousness.* New York: Seabury Press.

Graman, T. (1988). Education for humanization: Applying Paulo Friere's pedagogy to learning a second language. *Harvard Educational Review, 58*(4), 433-448.

Kazemek, F.E. (1988). Necessary change: Professional involvement in adult literacy programs. *Harvard Educational Review, 58*(4), 464-487.

Rigg, P. (1985). Petra: Learning to read at 45. *Journal of Education, 167*(1), 129-143.

Staton, J., Shuy, R.W., Peyton, J.K., & Reed, L. (1988). *Dialogue journal communication: Classroom, linguistic, social and cognitive views.* Norwood, NJ: Ablex.

Sticht, T. G. (1988). Adult literacy education. In E. Rothkopf (Ed.), *Review of research in education, Vol. 15.* Washington, DC: American Educational Research Association.

Vygotsky, L.S. (1986). *Thought and language.* Alex Kozulin (Ed. and Trans.). Cambridge, MA: M.I.T. Press. (Originally published in Moscow, 1934)

Vygotsky, L.S. (1978). *Mind in society: The development of higher psychological processes.* M. Cole, V. John, S. Scribner, E. Souberman (Eds. and Trans.). Cambridge, MA: Harvard University Press.

Dear Paul;
How are you Paul. I am a student. I am from Vietnam and my family have Five people. good bay Paul
Nguyen Hang

Dear Nguyen,
Thank you for your letter! You have a big family! I saw you in the morning with your children, on Eddy St. You have a nice family. I am not married, but I have a nice family. My sister and my parents live in San Francisco. Sincerely, Paul

Dear Paul;
I am very happy thank you for Paul. When you saw me on the eddy st. but, I don't know you. good bay Paul.
Nguyen Hang

Part I

An Introduction to Dialogue Journal Writing

Dialogue, of course, is nothing new. It is as old as animal and human communication, in whatever form. Written dialogue, though much more recent, is not a new idea either. Human beings have been communicating through pictures, notes, and letters since before the Ice Age. Written dialogue in the classroom, however, an idea that originated with teachers, is relatively new and has been taken seriously only in the past few years. Until recently, we tended not to think of writing as "dialogue," as involving a pair or group of voices, but more as performance—a solitary writer producing a finished text (maybe even a fill-in-the-blank paragraph) for a receiver who was not immediately present. We have learned, though, that there is nothing solitary about writing. Writers step into an ongoing stream of dialogue, of past and future thoughts exchanged orally and in writing. Educators are only beginning to explore the many forms that the exchange can take, within the classroom and around the world.

Dialogue journal writing is a simple, easy-to-implement educational idea, an open-ended communication that teachers and students have adapted and changed to suit their situations and meet their needs.

1

Dialogue journals can be used in any type of program with students of any age and proficiency level, working in their native languages or a second language. Students simply communicate at the level at which they are able and challenged.

Whether about students' own backgrounds, thoughts, and experiences, or about social or political topics or academic topics studied in school, the writing relates closely to the realities of students' lives. That is, they have the opportunity to reflect on ideas, experiences, and content, to get them out on paper, and to receive a reply that they also have time to reflect on and to digest. The physical privacy of writing and reading promote reflection and openness.

Although essentially a simple concept, there are important issues to be considered, questions to be answered, and details to be worked out by teachers and students embarking on a dialogue journal exchange. These are covered in the papers in this section. We have included one overview article in Spanish, which easily stands on its own as an introduction to dialogue journal use and can be used profitably in programs with Spanish-speaking teachers and students.

1

What Are Dialogue Journals?

Paul Jones
Putney, Vermont

Dialogue journals are essentially written conversations between a student and teacher, kept in a bound notebook or on a computer disk or file. Both partners write back and forth, frequently, and over a period of time, about whatever interests them. Their goal is to communicate in writing, to exchange ideas and information free of the concern for form and correctness so often imposed on developing writers.

In this chapter, the basic ingredients that distinguish dialogue journals from other forms of school-based writing are reviewed. Then, some of the qualities that give the genre its unique power as a teaching tool are presented. Finally, the diverse contexts in which dialogue journals can be used to help develop reading and writing abilities in students, in their first or second language, are described.

The Basic Ingredients

The name "dialogue journal" was coined in 1979 by educational psychologist Jana Staton and sixth-grade teacher Leslee Reed to describe Reed's practice of writing freely back and forth, every day, with each of her students (Staton & Peyton, 1990). Since then, and as the practice has become more widespread, linguists and educators have identified several essential ingredients that distinguish dialogue journal writing from other kinds of written communication.

First, dialogue journal writing is interactive. Teacher and student take equal turns writing and responding. Both partners write frequently, usually between one and three times weekly for adult students. The writing is sustained for anywhere from several months to a year, typically for the duration of a course (Kreeft, Staton, & Gutstein, 1984).

Topics are typically not assigned, leaving both participants free to discuss whatever they wish. The interaction thus becomes largely student generated. In some courses, such as literature, science, social studies, or advanced language study, students may be asked to address topics related to course content (Atwell, 1987; Staton, Peyton, & Gutstein, 1989; Walworth, 1990). Within that broad guideline, however, they have freedom to initiate, abandon, or expand on topics they choose.

As a rule, dialogue journals are not corrected, nor are they graded or evaluated. The absence of corrections is central to the creation of a genuine dialogue, yet it raises some thorny issues with adult students, related to accurate learning of the forms of a new language. These issues are examined in some detail in Part V. "Benefits for Students and Teachers."

Most teachers keep the writing private, promising not to show a journal to any third party without the student's consent, and then generally only for research or teacher training purposes, maintaining strict student anonymity.

Finally, the dialogue is preserved in some tangible, durable form that gives both writers ongoing and easy access to all that has transpired thus far. Although bound notebooks are most often used, other forms, such as computer disks or files, are also possible. Unlike oral conversations, dialogue journal interactions allow participants time to read, reread, and reflect on what has been said previously before responding (Kreeft, Staton, & Gutstein, 1984).

Qualities That Make a Difference

The basic ground rules of dialogue journal writing—that the writing be interactive, frequent, sustained, open-ended, not corrected, private, and somehow durable and accessible—set the stage for five more complex qualities that characterize many, if not all, dialogue journal exchanges. These five qualities set the genre apart dramatically from other kinds of scholastic writing and classroom interaction and give it its compelling power as a teaching tool.

First, the focus of the interaction is on real communication, not on form. Second, along with the privacy of the writing, the absence of corrections makes dialogue journals relatively nonthreatening to most students. Third, because the journals are individualized and largely student generated, they can capture and sustain remarkably high student interest. Fourth, teacher and student can act as relatively equal partners in the discourse, temporarily stepping out of their customarily hierarchical relationship. Fifth, the genre encourages students to express in writing a wide variety of language functions, such as reporting facts, making requests, complaining, giving excuses, predicting, and so on (Kreeft, Shuy, Staton, Reed, & Morroy, 1984; Staton, Shuy, Peyton, & Reed, 1988). Finally, the dialogue evolves over time, beginning with relatively simple, factual subjects and then moving on to topics of greater intimacy and sharing.

The interplay of these qualities is illustrated clearly in the dialogue journal writing of Nguyen Hang (this student granted permission to publish her sample using a pseudonym), a beginning ESL student in her early twenties. The following are the first three complete turns (student entry plus teacher response) from her journal, which was begun three weeks into the semester:

January 26

Dear Paul;

How are you Paul. I am a student. I am from Vietnam and my family have Five people. good bay Paul

Nguyen Hang

Dear Nguyen,

Thank you for your letter! You have a big family! I saw you in the morning before school with your children, on Eddy St. You have a nice family. I am not married, but I have a

5

nice family. My sister and my parents live in San Francisco.

Sincerely, Paul

January 27

Dear Paul,

I am very happy thank you for Paul. When you saw me on the eddy st. but, I don't know you. good bay Paul.

Nguyen Hang

Dear Nguyen

When I saw you on Eddy street, I was driving my car, so you could not see me. But you were walking, so I could see you. What are your children's names?

Sincerely, Paul

January 28

Dear Paul

Where are you going You saw me on Eddy Street. Hello Paul. You want know my family name. First Son _____. Second Son_____. and theeth my daughter name is _____. Good night. Paul see you again   see you again

Nguyen Hang

Dear Nguyen,

I was coming to school at about 7:30 in the morning when I saw you walking with your children, on Eddy St., near Van Ness St.

Sincerely, Paul

Focus on Communication

In these entries Nguyen talks about herself and her family, and then enters into an extended discussion about when, where, and why they were seen on the street. There are errors, such as the absence of punctuation for questions and of certain past tense verb forms, but they do not hinder the flow of the discussion. What counts is the message, and it gets across. Similarly, the question to Nguyen ("What are your children's names?") is real. The teacher is seeking information that he honestly does not know and is interested in, rather than simply trying to elicit correct usage of a particular grammatical structure. This letter format is not necessary, and many teachers and students omit the salutation and closing.

Nonthreatening

Nguyen was a shy student, rarely venturing to speak during the first month of class. In these initial entries to her dialogue journal, however, she opened up right away. Unlike some classroom activities from which she held back, the journal was clearly nonthreatening to her.

High Interest

The major topic in these entries, families, was initiated by Nguyen. The other major topic, Paul's morning sighting of Nguyen and her family, grew out of Paul's attempt to ask about her family. It is perhaps not surprising, then, that the dialogue journal consistently captured Nguyen's interest; she eagerly read and wrote in her journal every time it was given to her. As the semester progressed, she took obvious delight in telling all about her family, and in particular about her newborn daughter, subjects of great personal significance. She seemed equally interested in asking Paul questions of a somewhat personal nature.

Equality in the Interaction

There is a striking equality in this dialogue that seems radically different from a traditional, hierarchical teacher-student relationship. It seems like an initial chat between two newly acquainted peers. Each one talks about himself and asks questions about the other. During class, in contrast, Nguyen adopted a traditional student role, never asking questions and rarely discussing personal information, except as part of a planned class activity.

This dramatic shift to a relatively equal status in discourse is one of

7

the most striking dimensions of written dialogue. As linguist Robby Morroy has stated, the teacher seems to "camouflage her authority" to promote honest communication (Morroy, 1985, p. 62). Staton and her collaborators in the first major study of dialogue journals noted that through this equality, the teacher "shares the power to get things done in the classroom through writing with her students" (Staton, et al., 1988, p. 4). This equality, which also allows students to get to know their teacher as another human being rather than as an authority figure, certainly contributes to the captivating power of dialogue journals.

Functional

In these brief entries, Nguyen's writing demonstrates a variety of communicative purposes, or what some sociolinguists call "language functions" (Shuy, 1988). These include reporting personal facts ("I am a student"), responding to questions ("You want know my family name. First son ..."), requesting information ("Where are you going You saw me on Eddy St."), and thanking ("thank you for your"). In subsequent entries, Nguyen's writing exhibited a great many other functions as well, such as giving opinions ("I like San Francisco...night times very beautiful"); giving excuses ("I at home because my son sick"); expressing desires ("I am very like a dryer"); and complaining ("but I don't have a room keep a dryer"); and evaluating ("...you be my teacher very excellent, gave me know a lot many many thing"). Sociolinguist Roger Shuy has analyzed the language functions in the dialogue writing of numerous native and nonnative English speaking children and found at least fifteen major recurring language functions typical of the genre, including (in addition to those illustrated above) giving directives, apologizing, offering, predicting, and reporting and requesting various types of information (Shuy, 1988, p. 110).

Evolving over Time

Dialogue journal writing differs from oral conversation in that both participants have ample time to think about what they want to say between turns and to review what has already been said before responding. Yet, the interaction resembles spoken conversation in several ways. As in talks between friends, topics can run the gamut from mundane factual matters to more involved personal, political, or philosophical issues, depending on both participants' interests. Over several months following the initial entries shown above, for instance, the dialogue in Nguyen's journal covered such subjects as families, household life, food, Chinese and American holidays, San Francisco, work, movies, and dentists. Although Nguyen's initial writing tended to be reportorial, over time she increasingly expressed feelings and opinions as well. Likewise, studies of dialogue journal writing over time have found that written dialogue, like oral conversation between new friends, tends to evolve in stages, beginning with relatively simple, factual subjects and moving on eventually to greater intimacy and sharing (Lindfors, 1988; Staton, et al., 1988).

Conclusion

The six qualities demonstrated in Nguyen's journal entries, and consistently documented in the genre by linguists and educators, stand in stark contrast to much of traditional school-based writing, which tends to be more teacher generated, less consistently interesting to a wide variety of students, more heavily concerned with form and linguistic accuracy (Elbow, 1985), and often limited in the various types of expression elicited from students (Appleby, 1984).

Dialogue journals are more than simply an alternative to school-based writing. They involve students and teachers in an ongoing, nonhierarchical sharing of ideas that is usually meaningful and often captivating. Over time, as in spoken conversations, the dialogue tends to evolve from simple, impersonal subjects to more complex, sometimes personal themes.

These qualities give dialogue journals remarkable power to affect classroom relationships, to help shape teacher and student attitudes, and to foster in students the development of new language and writing skills. They can also serve as a useful planning and assessment tool for teachers and as an integral part of other types of writing done in class. Finally, they can even inspire and motivate teachers in their classroom teaching.

References

Appleby, A.N. (1984). *Contexts for learning to write: Studies of secondary school instruction*. Norwood, NJ: Albex.

Atwell, N. (1987). *In the middle: Writing, reading, and learning with adolescents*. Upper Montclair, NJ: Boynton/Cook.

Elbow, P. (1985). The shifting relationships between speech and writing. *College Composition and Communication, 36*, 283-303.

Kreeft, J., Staton, J., & Gutstein, S. (1984). What is dialogue? *Dialogue, 2*(1), 1.

Kreeft, J., Shuy, R.W., Staton, J., Reed, L., & Morroy, R. (1984). *Dialogue writing: Analysis of student-teacher interactive writing in the learning of English as a second language*. (NIE-G-83-0030). Washington, DC: Center for Applied Linguistics. (ERIC Document Reproduction Service No. ED 252 097)

Lindfors, J. W. (1988). From "talking together" to "being together in talk." *Language Arts, 65*(2), 135-141.

Morroy, R. (1985). *Teacher strategies: Linguistic devices for sustaining interaction in dialogue journal writing*. Unpublished doctoral dissertation, Georgetown University, Washington, DC.

Shuy, R. W. (1988). Sentence level language functions. In J. Staton, R.W. Shuy, J.K. Peyton, & L. Reed, (Eds.), *Dialogue journal communication: Classroom, linguistic, social and cognitive views* (pp. 107-142). Norwood, NJ: Ablex.

Staton, J., & Peyton, J. K. (1990). A history of dialogue journals (preface). *Dialogue, Back Issues from 1982-1989*. Washington, DC: Center for Applied Linguistics.

Staton, J., Peyton, J. K., & Gutstein, S. (Eds.). (1989). Dialogue in content area instruction: Promise and practice. *Dialogue, 6*(2).

Staton, J., Shuy, R. W., Peyton, J. K., & Reed, L. (1988). *Dialogue journal communication: Classroom, linguistic, social and cognitive views*. Norwood, NJ: Ablex.

Walworth, M. (1990). Interactive teaching of reading: A model. In J.K. Peyton (Ed.), *Students and teachers writing together: Perspectives on journal writing* (pp. 37-47). Washington, DC: Teachers of English to Speakers of Other Languages.

2

Settling Some Basic Issues

Joy Kreeft Peyton
Center for Applied Linguistics
Washington, DC

There are many issues and details to consider when starting and maintaining effective dialogue journal interaction with students developing language and literacy skills. These details include when, where, and how often to write; what to write in; which topics to write about; how to introduce the idea to students; how to keep the dialogue going; and how to work with students of different ages and levels of English proficiency. These issues are covered in depth in many different publications (see Dialogue Journal Resources, this volume; Peyton & Reed, 1990) and do not need to be repeated here. However, writing with adults does raise new issues that deserve special attention. Addressed here are those issues frequently raised by practitioners contemplating or attempting to use dialogue journals with nonnative English speaking adults at various stages of literacy development whether in their native language or in English (see Gross, 1990; Jones, 1988, for discussions of dialogue journal start-up and maintenance issues to be considered when working with adults, and Wigfield, this volume, for some questions the practice raises and some alternative models for implementation). These include managing time, "correcting" student writing, working with beginning literates, maintaining confidentiality and privacy, integrating dialogue journal writing into the literacy program, and creating an authentic partnership.

Managing Time

One of the first issues that comes up in discussions of dialogue journal writing is the amount of time it takes the teacher to read and write in students' journals. Writing to students night after night, in addition to reviewing other student work and preparing for the next class, can become exhausting. The more proficient students become as writers, the more demanding the reading and writing is for the teacher. Janet Gross, for example, teaching English to adult students in Madrid, became temporarily overwhelmed with her work load and let her writing lapse. Her students soon made their dissatisfaction known:

> *"I don't like to write letter if any people don't answer me."*
>
> *"Listen, Janet, if you don't answer me I will tell you nothing more because this can get in a monologue and this is very bored."*
>
> (Gross, 1990, p. 54)

Teachers who think the dialogue is important to them and their students usually find the time, just as they find the time for other important parts of their programs. Teachers have worked out many different strategies to manage the work load that written dialogue inevitably creates. Some write with only a few of their classes (no one can write with 100 students every day!); others ask students to write only twice or three times a week; others respond to every two student entries rather than every one (for example, Gross' students write on Mondays, Tuesdays, Thursdays, and Fridays; on Tuesdays and Fridays they can continue their Monday and Thursday entries or begin a new one; she responds on Wednesdays and weekends); others combine teacher-student and student-student writing or share the work with a classroom aide. Teachers need to find ways that are manageable for them, so they can enjoy the dialogue and maintain the integrity of rich interaction.

Correcting Student Writing

The issue of correcting student writing arises with all students, but seems to be of particular concern when working with adults, who are often preoccupied with the desire to write everything correctly. While this important student concern needs to be taken seriously and honored, it also needs to be discussed and placed in a proper perspective. Students who have been conditioned by their educational experiences to think that written expression involves producing perfect final text, without surface errors, for evaluation by a teacher, need to understand that much more is involved. Writing also involves exploring ideas for one's own understanding, finding a personal voice and appropriate style to express those ideas, reworking ideas, and experimenting with ways to make them interesting and compelling to a reader. In fact, concern with grammatical accuracy and correct punctuation and capitalization comes rather late in the writing process. Dialogue journal writing is one place where students can engage freely in written thought with an interested and attentive audience.

At the same time, students need to be reassured that proper attention will indeed be paid to their grammar and syntax. This might occur primarily in other extended writing they do, which is revised and edited until a clean product is achieved, or in exercises that focus on aspects of grammar and syntax. Some teachers also attend to correct written forms in the journals, without inhibiting the dialogue, by one or more of the following means:

1.   Modeling correct usage in their responses. This entails modeling the student's usage in the context of genuine communication, as in this example from the journal of a beginning student (from Spener, this volume):

> *Mi mothar she liv en Cochabamba.*
>
> *You say your mother lives in Cochabamba. Who does she live with there? My mother lives in New York City. She lives with my father, my grandmother, and my little brother.*

2.   Taking note of problem areas common to many students and addressing them separately, in a class minilesson.

3.   Holding periodic individual conferences with students in which teacher and student review a page from the student's journal, identifying errors, and discussing relevant rules and corrections.

4.   Adding a "grammatical P.S." at the end of a student's entry, a gentle note about a couple of specific points: "By the way, in English we usually say..." (Jones, 1988, p. 66).

Even with these nonintrusive methods of "correcting," it is important to convey to the students that their errors are not being pointed out because they are expected to write correctly. They are expected to write meaningfully, and their journal writing provides a context for examining various aspects of the form of their writing.

Working with Beginning Literates

Many literacy programs have adult students who are not only nonliterate in English but also have little or no literacy background in their native language. Many teachers have asked, how can these students keep a dialogue journal? My answer always is that if first graders learning English can do it (see Peyton, 1990), why can't adults? Once students have some proficiency with oral English, and some familiarity with English print, they can begin. They will of course not begin reading and writing long messages, but they can communicate something. Before they are able to write very much, they might do the following:

- **Draw.** Although many educators working with adults feel that it is demeaning to ask adults to draw (an option that is always available, and widely used, with children), some adults do in fact draw all or parts of their entries until they become more facile with print. The teacher or an aide can write a reply about the picture, and read it to the student.
- **Dictate.** Adults can dictate their message to a teacher, aide, or other student. Their message can then be read aloud, a reply written, and the reply read aloud.

- **Write**. Adults can write whatever they do know and let the teacher complete the rest. Dan Rabideau (this volume), for example, asks students to write the first letter of words they don't know and put a line (e.g., J ___). He then fills in these words for them.

Gradually the students build up a body of written text to draw on for future entries and begin to recognize and produce more words independently. (See also Spener, this volume, for strategies for working with beginning writers, and Davis, this volume, for a description of one student's development.) Students who are literate in their own language can begin by writing their journal entries in that language (if the teacher, aide, or another student knows it), and gradually move to English.

An obvious but often overlooked fact is that all of us learned to speak by first making unconnected sounds, gradually producing a new word at a time, and building from there. Our sounds and words generated language from others on which we built increasingly complex and sophisticated language. There is no reason that writing cannot proceed in the same way.

Maintaining Confidentiality and Privacy

It is important with students of all ages to assure them that their writing will not be shared with others unless they choose to share it, and to staunchly honor this promise. Adult students seem especially sensitive to this issue. Janet Gross (1990) stumbled onto this important realization by accident. Attempting to encourage collaboration in her class, she asked her beginning ESL writers in Vermont to share what they had written in their journals with a partner before turning it in to her.

> To my surprise, they refused, quite emphatically telling me the journals were confidential. I hadn't thought that describing a weekend in New York or sharing what they ate the night before in the cafeteria was private. This underestimation of their investment in our one-on-one partnership was never repeated.

> (Gross, 1990, p. 120)

15

If the teacher wants to use examples of student writing in articles or presentations, it is important to get permission both orally and in writing, making it clear that the student is free to refuse permission without negative consequences. Students should also be able to choose whether or not they want their real name used. Some students wish to be identified, even by first and last name, and should be given that opportunity. Others wish not to. Janet Isserlis (personal communication, May, 1990) uses the following form for written permission.

My teacher, _____, has my permission
to use examples of my writing when she writes articles for teachers about literacy and learning English.
She can:

_____ Use my stories/writing.

_____ Use my name.

_____ She should not use my stories/writing.

_____ She should not use my name.

Signed, _____ Date _____

Closely related to the issues of privacy and confidentiality is that of ownership. The journals belong to the students, and they should be free to keep them when they are full. As David Spener (this volume) suggests, the journals represent an important part of their lives, and they and even their grandchildren might enjoy reading them years later.

Integrating Dialogue Journal Writing in the Literacy Program

Dialogue journal writing does not constitute an entire writing program, because it does not encompass all aspects of the writing process. Students also need to do extended writing that they rework, revise, and edit; they need to write in various styles, forms, and genres, both formal and informal, about both personal and academic topics.

They may also need to spend some time focusing on particular grammatical structures or other work- and sentence-level features of written language.

At the same time, this type of writing is very important. In a recent study comparing various pieces of in-class writing of ESL students (Peyton, Staton, Richardson, & Wolfram, 1990), dialogue journal writing was found to show greater complexity and variety on several linguistic measures than other pieces. We concluded that while students learning English as a second language need many and varied opportunities to do formal, content-based, nonpersonal writing, they may not be able to use the full range of their language abilities in these contexts. In order to display and stretch their expressive abilities, students also need opportunities to explore topics and styles that they find appealing, and in their own ways.

Laura Klos Sokol, Janet Isserlis, and Loren McGrail (this volume) describe the ways they have integrated dialogue journal writing into their program, by using the dialogue journal texts as starting places for class discussions, further reading, and more formal writing about issues of concern to students.

Creating an Authentic Partnership

In studies of dialogue journal writing over the past ten years, the changed nature of the student-teacher relationship in the context of this kind of writing has always been very salient. The teacher becomes a partner in a shared dialogue. Sometimes, when the interaction is particularly successful, traditional hierarchical student-teacher roles seem suspended completely and a relationship of equality created, such as the "mutual conversations" found by Staton (1988) in some of the writing of a sixth-grade teacher and her students:

> ...mutual conversations [are] those instances in the
> dialogue writing in which both writers jointly con-
> struct a topic of such importance that both can con-
> tribute new information about it, and converse as

17

> equals for an extended series of turns. The student in such conversations often takes on the adult's role of directing the interchanges, and the teacher takes on the student's role of responding with new information. The classroom roles of student and teacher are temporarily transcended as they adopt new roles of two colleagues exploring a mutually interesting topic. Both become teachers, both learners.

(Staton, 1988, p. 30)

The possibility of a changed, more equal student-teacher relationship seems to be a crucial element in programs for adults, who are working, functional members of our society, who are equal to their teachers in many areas, and who depend on the teacher simply for the learning of oral and written English. As others in this volume, following Freire (1970), have pointed out, a "banking" approach to education, in which the teacher attempts to fill students with knowledge and periodically checks to make sure the knowledge is in fact "getting in," a questionable enough approach with children, is particularly unsuccessful with adults. Adults especially need to work through and negotiate knowledge with others who respect them as equals and partners in teaching and learning. They need to "find and elaborate their own generative themes and to connect their existential experience to the world of those whose language they are learning" (Graman, 1988, p. 444).

Written interactions in dialogue journals seem perfectly suited for such a relationship. But does this kind of relationship actually occur in the writing? Are student-teacher roles really changed? Or are accepted and comfortable hierarchies carried on, but simply in written form? In the case of the adult developing literacy, is the unfortunate dynamic of the knowing teacher working with the dependent illiterate being perpetuated? These questions have been explored with tremendous insight by two dialogue journal teacher/researchers. Judith Lindfors (1988), in her written interactions with a class of Zulu students (ages 12-16) in South Africa, distinguishes between "talking together," a minimal level of communicating together—sharing ideas, learning from each other, attempting to understand each other, and keeping the interaction going—and "being together in talk," when both partners are completely engaged in the writing, are free to be themselves, and are not struggling to keep something going, but instead letting it unfold and develop of its own accord because both are fully engaged in the topic. Her writing with one student, MM, illustrating "talking together," is probably typical of the written interaction that goes on in many dialogue journal classrooms.

> *I am a beautiful boy and title. My name is MM. I am talking about this clentis wood [Clint Eastwood?] I am crazy about that man who play films and it was the dangerous man in the world. Sometimes me I play a beautiful films.*
>
> *You must tell me more about Clentis Wood. Who is he? What does he do that makes him the most dangerous man in the world?*

Judith went on to ask MM whether he watched television, particularly "Dallas" and "The A Team," and closed with, "I look forward to your telling me more about your hero, Clentis Wood." Reflecting on that interaction later, she confesses:

> It would have been closer to the truth to say, "I want you to keep writing to me, and I'm using Clentis Wood (like 'Dallas' and 'The A Team') as an enticement" ...the simple truth is that I am not interested in Clentis Wood, J. R., or The A Team, and writing about these was not engaging me. These topics were simply the means to the end I cared very much about: sustaining a written conversation with MM .
>
> (Lindfors, 1988, p. 137)

At times, Lindfors and the students were able to "be together in talk." Sometimes these interactions revolved around shared humor, or shared involvement in a fairly mundane task, or an intensely personal experience that both were genuinely interested in. The example below shows part of one such interaction that continued for several days.

> *Student*
>
> *which birds do you know? you know swallow, it is maroon in colour. I hope you know it. you know the eagle the biggest*

bird in the world it eat flesh (meat). that bird can kill a man. It has sharp claws, sharp mouth. that is the dangerous bird. another one is ostrich. it has long legs. that one eats snakes and the babies of crocodile. another one is owl. the owl is waking only at the night during the day it sleeps. It has big eyes. I think it sees clearly only at night

have a nice day Madam

I'll continue next time

Judith

We have some sayings about owls and ostriches. People in America say that owls are very wise. They think that owls look wise in their appearance. So if someone is a very clever person, others may say, "He is as wise as an owl." Ostriches sometimes bury their heads in the sand. In America one person may say to another, "Don't be an ostrich and bury your head in the sand." This means that the person is not paying attention. The person is ignoring information that he should be noticing.

Student

As I promised you last time to continue by counting birds. Do you know the dove. I hope you know it. It is blue in colour. Sparrow I think you

Judith

Yes, I do know the dove. Did you know that the dove is the symbol for peace? In the States you often see the dove pictured on Christmas cards. The message (words) will be something about peace. In 1983 I was in the Soviet Union for a week. In Moscow I went to a store that sold posters. Many of them had pictures of a dove too, with a message about peace....

This kind of interaction did not happen with all of the students and the texts were not always lofty or inspired, but it did happen, and when real dialogue did take place, it was clear that there was a different quality to the writing.

Similarly, Janet Gross, teaching adult ESL students in Vermont, many the same age or older than she was, found that while she was in one sense writing as a dialogue partner, sharing ideas, problems, observations, and experiences, she was at the same time still very much acting as a language teacher—watching the students' language and attempting to model correct usage; requesting clarification of students' contributions; and "playing the interviewer" with questions intended to advance the dialogue and strengthen the student's ability to communicate clearly.

As she continued to write, though, she began to feel that her continual attempts to model the students' language for them reflected a lack of trust in them and their abilities to learn from their interactions with others.

> My covert grammar manipulations revealed a lack of faith and respect in my partners' learning abilities and an overpowering need on my part to control the language acquisition component of our dialogue. I was unwilling to let them learn whatever they might pick up from my entries.
>
> (Gross, 1990, pp. 109-110)

Like Lindfors, she discovered in her requests for clarification and information more a desire to keep the dialogue going, to keep the student writing, than a desire to know what the student really thought.

> Was I asking for clarification about something I really didn't know and wanted to know, or was I asking to guide the student toward correction?... I am not sure

that a role reversal which allows the student to fill the teacher with information, thoughts and experiences (in answer to the teacher's questions) with little reciprocity is not as patronizing as the more traditional role.... My entries did not reflect me or my interests. They reflected someone trying to keep the dialogue moving. I was neutral.

(Gross, 1990, pp. 109-110)

Gross decided that as long as she concentrated solely on the students' learning she was prevented from participating fully in the dialogue. Her most effective writing occurred when she was not attempting to improve students' language learning, but was simply a fellow participant, an interested native speaker; when "my dialogue partner and I became human beings learning from each other, both working to create an understandable text made specifically for and by each other" (p. 126).

The experiences of these two teachers demonstrate clearly that simply writing in a dialogue journal with students does not mean that hierarchical student-teacher relationships will necessarily change or that "mutual conversations," "being together in talk," will automatically occur. As much as we might desire them, these changes, these new dynamics, can take a lot of time and may fly in the face of years of our own educational conditioning. In some cases, they will not take place at all. At the same time, they are worth striving for, for they signal a genuine, fertile context for learning and growing. Since others have identified the pitfalls for us, we need to watch out for them in our own writing, work through them, and cultivate the times when we are simply communicating freely, as fellow human beings.

References

Freire, P. (1970). *Pedagogy of the oppressed*. New York: Seabury Press.

Graman, T. (1988). Education for humanization: Applying Paulo Freire's pedagogy to learning a second language. *Harvard Educational Review, 58*(4), 433-448.

Gross, J. F. (1990). *Learning partnership through dialogue journals: Applying non-hierarchic assumptions in the classroom*. Unpublished Master's thesis, School for International Training, Brattleboro, VT.

Jones, P. M. (1988). *Knowing opportunities: Some possible benefits and limitations of dialogue journals in adult second language instruction*. Unpublished Master's thesis. School for International Training, Brattleboro, VT.

Lindfors, J. W. (1988). From "talking together" to "being together in talk." *Language Arts, 65*(2), 135-141.

Peyton, J. K. (1990). Beginning at the beginning: First grade ESL students learn to write. In A. M. Padilla, H. H. Fairchild, & C. M. Valadez (Eds.), *Bilingual education: Issues and strategies* (pp. 195-218). Newbury Park: Sage.

Peyton, J. K. (1988). Mutual conversations: Written dialogue as a basis for building student-teacher rapport. In J. Staton, R. W. Shuy, J. K. Peyton, & L. Reed (Eds.), *Dialogue journal communication: Classroom, linguistic, social and cognitive views* (pp. 183-201). Norwood, NJ: Ablex.

Peyton, J. K., & Reed, L. (1990). *Dialogue journal writing with nonnative English speakers: A handbook for teachers*. Washington, DC: Teachers of English to Speakers of Other Languages.

Peyton, J. K., Staton, J., Richardson, G., & Wolfram, W. (1990). The influence of writing tasks on ESL students' written production. *Research in the Teaching of English, 24*(2), 142-172.

Staton, J. (1988). An introduction to dialogue journal communication. In J. Staton, R. W. Shuy, J. K. Peyton, & L. Reed (Eds.), *Dialogue journal communication: Classroom, linguistic, social and cognitive views* (pp. 1-32). Norwood, NJ: Ablex.

3

Dialogue Journals and ESL Adult Literacy: Some Questions to Consider

Jack Wigfield
 Alemany Community College Center
San Francisco, California

ESL literacy acquisition involves learning to read and write in English, the individual's second, or weaker language. For some, it may mean learning to read and write for the first time in any language. Some practitioners in ESL adult literacy believe that students should use their literacy skills as soon as possible, however primitive their efforts. In order for this to happen, the teacher must provide many opportunities for the students actually to read and write and then provide some kind of response to what the students have produced.

Several basic principles are applied in many early literacy classes. First, students are encouraged to use block printing (LIKE THIS). Block printing is relatively easy to learn because there are no capitalization rules, and the letters are made up of a small number of strokes or features that can be grouped and taught as a unit (D-P-B-R, for example). There is no above-the-line/below-the-line confusion. Block printing is socially acceptable, commonly used, and the only internationally standardized Roman script.

Second, students' "interlanguages," their approximation of the target language, based on their knowledge of their first language or the oral forms of the written language, are built on as valuable resources for writing. This is the principle that underlies the Language Experience Approach (LEA), and it is especially important with ESL students, because interlanguages account for various stages of vocabulary and grammar development as well as for cultural background and interests, all of which might be very heterogeneous in an ESL class.

Third, the whole literacy process begins with writing, which in a short time gives way to much more rapid development of reading skills. The two draw from and build on each other. Finally, teachers react, as much as possible in writing, to the content of students' writing, not only to prove to them that they actually are communicating, but to show them that the teacher enjoys reading their writing.

Where does journal writing fit into the overall approach? Most important, journal writing of any kind allows beginning literacy learners to write the easiest form of exposition, a narrative, a stream-of-consciousness account—who, what, where, and when. Students can begin to write in a journal as soon as they have acquired a rudimentary ability to convey meaning in print. Journals allow learning to take place on a highly individual basis—students write what and how they know best. Keeping a journal motivates them to write, and they come to class looking for their journals. They may have done some prewriting on the way to school (thinking through what they want to say, maybe jotting down some notes), and now are ready to put it all down. However, the use of journal writing in the ESL adult literacy classroom also raises some questions that need to be thought through.

The first issue has to do with *the type of journal to be used*. Journals can be effective when treated as personal diaries, a convention common in many cultures. A diary is an internal dialogue. In this form it may remain the very personal possession of the student. Why else are diary books sold with a lock and key? But if a diary-journal is totally personal, for the student's use only, how does the teacher become involved in and help with the process of literacy development? Is it enough to let students write to please themselves? Is the student's personal satisfaction with having written something enough? Or does the teacher need to be involved in some way?

This leads to the second issue, that of *the nature of the teacher's involvement, or intervention*. The literature on dialogue journal writing, in which the teacher takes an active role as co-writer, is extensive as is evident by the Dialogue Journal Resources list at the end of this volume.

Teacher approaches and strategies are becoming more and more varied and sophisticated. But how do teachers find time to write comments for a class of over 30 students as well as plan for other classes? Do the rewards balance out the time spent? How do the surface features of students' writing get dealt with? Are students just left to discover grammatical rules and writing conventions themselves? Or are journals the place where teachers see the discrepancy between what they "taught" and what the students have learned? Are journals more diagnostic than treatment?

There is also the issue of *the medium for the writing*. The most commonly discussed medium for dialogue journal writing is a bound notebook of some sort. If a journal is an act of written communication, why does a notebook have to be used? Why not follow the usual convention of a letter or a note? Can't returned letters, letters that the teacher has responded to, be collected in a loose-leaf binder and serve the same purpose as a notebook? Or, would the letter medium create a separation that would break the ongoing relationship that a dialogue journal is trying to build? Is the physical journal important in itself?

There is also the issue of *the participants in the dialogue*. If written communication and response are our goals, is it more expedient to have students write to each other, rather than always writing to the teacher? Teachers of large classes might let other students do the reacting, while the teacher simply watches for those areas where students need help. The idea of pen pals is an old one, but is one that is experiencing a revival in numerous cross-age tutoring projects. Can't students write to upper-class students within their own school, or to students in another school in the same city, or anywhere? Letters elicit questions and comments from the reader that help the writer answer the ever-present question, "What should I write about?"

But, how do teachers of adults in open-enrollment schools manage pen pal exchanges? In such schools, there is a constant adding and dropping of students. Don't some students end up writing and not getting an answer? Do upper-level students *want* to correspond with someone who will write back simply and haltingly? Do those upper-level students accept the statement that they are learning by teaching? It may be that the journal is ultimately easier when treated as a self-contained, uncomplicated single-class activity.

Finally, there is the question of *the transfer of skills*. Does dialogue journal writing promote reading and writing skills that transfer to survival and competency tasks? Are journal writers better able to fill out forms, for example? Can journal writers communicate better with their children's teachers? Are the income tax forms of journal writers more accurate? Do journal writers have less trouble managing their gas and electric bills? That is, does journal writing lead to more effective functioning in these practical aspects of the student's world?

The use of journal writing in ESL adult literacy classes, particularly dialogue journals, may on the surface appear to be an easy decision. But, this decision needs to be thought through carefully in light of the questions raised above. The answers to these questions will determine not only whether and how journal writing is to be implemented, but how successful it will be in accomplishing the goals of the teacher and the students.

4

El Cuaderno de Diálogos: La Alfabetización a Través de Conversaciones Escritas

Dan Rabideau
Literacy Assistance Center
New York, NY

En los Centros de Alfabetización de la Biblioteca Pública de Nueva York, creemos que los estudiantes deben escribir desde el principio. Es una destreza que se desarrolla al mismo tiempo que se desarrolla la lectura. No nos preocupamos por la ortografía hasta más tarde en el proceso. Queremos que los estudiantes entiendan la escritura como una comunicación de ideas, no como listas de palabras que no tienen significado personal para ellos.

En este artículo, quisiera sugerir que el "Cuaderno de Diálogos"—conversaciones entre el estudiante y el maestro que se escriban en un cuaderno—ofrece una actividad en que las destrezas de la alfabetización pueden desarrollarse en una manera natural.

Joy Kreeft Peyton (1986), del Center for Applied Linguistics en Washington, DC, describe el cuaderno de diálogos como "un cuaderno en el cual el maestro y el estudiante se comunican regularmente—diariamente si es posible—por escrito. Los estudiantes escriben lo más que puedan sobre cualquier tema, y el maestro responde a cada estudiante como coparticipante en una conversación escrita, haciendo preguntas, respondiendo a las preguntas de los estudiantes, haciendo comentarios, pero jamás corrigiendo (la gramática u ortografía) (p. 24).

El siguiente ejemplo viene del cuaderno de una señora después de siete meses de haber empezado en el curso. (Es un curso de alfabetización para personas cuyo primer idioma es el inglés, pero el proceso es igual en cualquier idioma.) Nos dio permiso para copiar estas páginas. (Hemos copiado el diálogo sin correcciones.)

May 9, 1988

Teacher

I guess you didn't have time to write on Thursday. The hardest part of writing is finding something to write about.

I write about the books I am reading. I write about when I came to New York. I write about my family. I write about when I was small.

Can you think of other things to write about?

May 10, 1988

Student

I can Tell you about when i come to new yorkI way to Live with my husbond family i didn't have no Place To Live When i got a job i Found mine on Place. and i was very haPPy

Teacher

I bet you were glad to get your own place. What year did you come to New York? I came to New York in 1974. We lived in an old house in Brooklyn That old house didn't have any water and it didn't have any heat. It was a cold winter. What was your apartment like? What kind of job did you get?

May 11, 1988

Student

I came to New York and ,19,40 and I got a job in a Laundry

I was worked on a machine I was Pressing shirTs i was a pery worked i got pay by ther pery and I worked hard to make money for my family be my husband was very sick

Teacher

Yes. Piece work is very hard. You have to work fast if you want to make any money doing piece work. That was hard for you to take care of your family. Was your husband sick for a long time?

May 18, 1988

Teacher

I hope your hand is better today.

Student

Yes. My hand feel must better to day thin yeasday. I had to keep working for my family so we could have something to eat and a Place to stay and clothes to wear because my husband was sick and i had to KeeP worked.

May 19, 1988

Teacher

I know how that is. When I was small, my mother had to work. We were lucky. Our grandmother and our aunts and uncles helped us out. We were a very close family. Did you have anybody to help you out? Those were hard times for you. How many kids did you have?

Student

I have 3 kids and 1 die I have a body and a gril and thay or grown and married and thay have kids and they boy he have 4 kids 1 boy and 3 gril and the gril she have 6 kids and she have 3 gril and 3 boy

Teacher

You must be proud of your children and your grandchildren. Do you see your grandchildren often? Where do they live?

Las Ventajas del Cuaderno de Diálogos

Las ventajas del cuaderno de diálogos son varias. Al utilizar estos cuadernos en mi curso, he encontrado todas las ventajas que menciona la Sra. Peyton en su artículo.

- La escritura es funcional—da y recibe información.
- La estudiante ve la escritura como proceso, desarrolla y revisa de acuerdo con la reacción del lector. El 11 de mayo la estudiante en el ejemplo escribió acerca de sus experiencias cuando llegó a Nueva York. El 18 de mayo siguió explicando por qué tuvo que seguir trabajando.
- Este ejemplo conlleva un problema en particular en que el maestro introdujo los temas, pero espero que más adelante la estudiante tome la iniciativa de introducir nuevos temas. Sin embargo, el intercambio utiliza temas que son verdaderos para la estudiante. Esta actividad me ofrece la oportunidad de conocer a los estudiantes individualmente y abre más caminos de comunicación.
- El cuaderno se puede usar con los estudiantes a todo nivel de habilidad. Cuando trabajo con un principiante, le digo que escriba la primera letra de las palabras que no sabe escribir y que ponga una raya. Después, le ayudo a completar las palabras. Le explico que es para poder leer con más facilidad después. Poco a poco el estudiante va conociendo cada vez más palabras. Y puede reconocer más palabras en mi respuesta a su carta. (Trato de usar un lenguaje simple cuando le escribo a un principiante, pero mi primera meta es escribir lo que quiero comunicarle sin usar un lenguaje demasiado artificial.) También uso el cuaderno con los estudiantes a un nivel más avanzado.
- El cuaderno nos da prueba del progreso que está logrando el estudiante durante el año. Es importante para aquellos días cuando el

estudiante me dice, "Ay Mister, yo no siento que estoy progresando mucho." Revisamos el cuaderno y el estudiante (y yo también) nos asombramos cuando vemos que al principio apenas podía poner dos o tres garabatos en el cuaderno.

Notas

Este artículo fue adaptado, con permiso, de *El Español en Marcha*, 2(1), 7-8, December, 1988.
Comité de Educación Básica en Español
c/o Adult Education Program
Union Settlement Association
237 East 104th Street
New York, NY 10029
Attn: María Quiroga

Obras Citadas

Peyton, J. K. (1986). Literacy through written interaction. *Passage: A Journal for Refugee Education*, 2(1), 24-29.

WE READ TONIGHT WAS A STORY ABOUT spiderman
I THINK THE writ did good Job
THE STORY WAS INI
My SISTER HAVE A BOY 13 YEAR
HE LIKE HERO TOO. HE READ BOOK
AND HAVE Toyles TOO.
SO I HAVE a NICE TIME THIS
STORY   END

Dear Sammy,
    It sounds like you think the
story was interesting, and the
writer did a good job. How does a
writer do this?   Sara

A WRITE does a good Job
By USEING REAL THINGS AND PEOPLE
ALSO By write ABOUT THING
THAT HAPPEN IN REAL LIFE
I THINK IT is INTERESTING
WENT THE STORY is ABOUT
all KIND OF PEOPLE AND PLACE . . .

Part II

Different Ways of Using Dialogue Journals

For this section, we asked adult literacy educators who have used dialogue journals to describe their different practices with adult ESL learners, in the context of particular classroom or learning settings. This section offers readers an active debate about the concept of dialogue journals and contrasts various approaches to actual use in learning situations.

These accounts clearly demonstrate that dialogue journals fit naturally into a learner-centered curriculum, in which all the classroom methods build on students' life experiences and concerns. This is no coincidence, we suspect, but a natural alliance of compatible practices. The diversity of perspectives demonstrates how much the teacher shapes and makes possible the successful dialogue journal use, and challenges some basic assumptions. For example, Smokey Wilson found that tape-recorded dialogues worked much better than a written exchange for engaging her beginning students in dialogues about their reading.

What seems to unite these diverse contributions and differences of approach is the underlying "attitude of dialogue" and respect for the learner's knowledge and intelligence.

5

Between Teacher and Student: The Making of Texts by Adult New Readers

Smokey Wilson
Laney College
Oakland, California

Jenny Cook-Gumperz (1986) reminds us that literacies are socially constructed, a complex set of abilities that we learn in social settings. Several authors have recently described classrooms in which the social and collaborative nature of literacy drives the teaching practice (Atwell, 1987; Graves, 1990; Walworth, 1990). These classrooms encourage students to bring unique, personal interpretations to what they read, and the teacher contributes to and supports their interpretations. Such involvement with and interaction about text is vital, particularly when readers have experienced years of failure or are adults facing American culture and the English language for the first time, and are not confident about their ability to understand texts written in English. The challenge is to help these students become involved in making meaning of print.

It is important to recall that a view of literacy learning as inherently social and collaborative is a relatively new idea. In many discussions from the 1970s, the solitary writer was the image. As Rosen (1971) has pointed out, the writer was conceptualized as "a lonely figure...condemned to monologue" (p. 143). It has been only in the last few years that we have shifted from "an individual focus of 'what a person says' to a social focus of 'what people say to one another' " (Bleich, 1989; p. 38). In the same way, the shift away from the notion that there is only one "right" answer to comprehension questions has given way to the idea of multiple allowable interpretations of a text.

In the following pages, I describe one strategy that has allowed me to promote the social, collaborative aspects of literacy development and to share texts with students in a productive way. In the process of developing this strategy, I had to make fundamental changes in my approach to teaching reading. I found that my view of my students as inaccurate receivers of knowledge, which was "proven" by their low reading comprehension scores, did not foster active participation in reading. When I gave up the notion that a reading passage bears one specific message, packaged in a main idea and a set of details and inferences, that have to be reproduced almost verbatim in the student's mind, my students began to trust their interpretations of texts more fully. These changes in my basic orientation—away from "individual" reading tasks that involved answering "detail," "inference," and "main idea" questions correctly and toward a more collaborative classroom—naturally led to adjustments in the kinds of work I asked students to undertake. I began to read *with* students rather than teaching reading *to* them. I organized interest-based reading tasks and peer reading groups, and read individually with each student at least once a week. I also abandoned the multiple choice comprehension checks at the end of each reading passage.

These adjustments helped. But, although reading with peers served some beneficial functions, in many students' minds team reading did not fully replace the teacher's concentrated attention and support, and a heavy class load made it difficult to sustain collaborative reading relationships with each student during our one-hour class periods. Discontent grew—mine and theirs. I needed a way to look more closely at their reading processes. How could I foster the bookish intimacy I was seeking?

I had tried written dialogue journals and letters about reading, but had found these activities revealed very little about students' reading processes. I decided therefore to launch a tape-recorded reading journal. Students brought an audiotape, selected one or two paragraphs from a reading that they found meaningful that week, and read their selection into a tape recorder. Then they added their own comments about the reading, telling me what it meant to them and asking any questions they wanted answered. Deaf students who used signs rather than voice videotaped their reading and comments. I listened to (or viewed) each student's weekly recording and recorded my response, commenting on the ideas that the passage brought up for me, noting strengths in their reading of it, making suggestions for the next taping session, and answering questions. What began as stiff and formal "perfect performances" by students fearful of making even a single error soon became relaxed discussions between us—about books, characters, words, politics. As one student said, "We are reading and talking about life, right?"

These tape recordings have become a spoken dialogue journal, similar to written dialogue journals about books, described by Atwell (1987), Graves (1990), and Walworth (1990). This tape-recorded dialogue journal seems an inviting way for tentative students to begin to communicate about what they are reading and for more advanced and aggressive students to engage in deeper reflection. The journal is also valuable for the rich web of interaction it fosters—between teacher and student, student and text, text and teacher. In the tape-recorded journals students have access to the teacher's spontaneous ideas, individual instruction, and support. The teacher has access to each student's concerns, interests, and reading strategies. Through this process, we mutually construct a new text, a text that belongs to both of us.

When students read diffidently or haltingly, reading a passage on tape necessarily entails unfamiliar and possibly threatening moments. Yet, for those who take the risk, the rewards are considerable. The reading of one student in particular, Arlene, emphasizes the importance of risk taking in developing a new reader's engagement with text.

Arlene's multicultural background, Hawaiian, Puerto Rican, Spanish, and African-American, illustrates the wealth of language styles within which she operates. Yet, in spite of her broadly based language heritage, a sense of dread connected with previous school failures left her fearful of her future as a reader. Arlene's increasing involvement with her reading and growing willingness to take risks shows clearly in her tape recorded journal.

Her first reading was the semi-obligatory recitation of the previous day's classroom assignment, and my first response consisted of the equally ritualized advice that she could read anything she wanted, but that she needed to relax. For her second taped reading, she chose to read a story written by another student in her class about learning to drive in order to feel independent. In line with the author's main point, one might expect Arlene, who didn't drive, to express her desire to drive so that she could also become more independent and rely less on her 20-year-old daughter. However, she selected another theme for the focus of her interpretation:

> *...I don't drive. Lotta times I have the nerve to get up and do it but then I back away. Like everything else, you have to take that first step and maybe someday I'll end up taking that step to drive too.*
>
> *Like everything else, I'm nervous to drive. I don't find myself doing that.*

In my response to her, I interpreted her reference to learning to drive as a metaphor for the task of learning to read, and supported her struggle to try something new:

> *Learning how to drive is no joke. You might want to try some things that help you get over your nervousness. I am really impressed that you are trying so hard to learn to read when I know it makes you nervous.*

A few weeks later, Arlene selected a new text for the taping, a class handout called "History of English." In her interpretation of it, she gave a new twist to her developing theme of questions about herself as a reader:

> *... I'm finding out more and more each day that I read that I understand English more, and the more I read the more I like it. There's a lot more for me to learn, but it's a start, and I think I'm headed in the right direction. And that's why I picked this story. The story "History of English" is very fascinating to read.*

It seemed to make little difference what Arlene read, personal experience or history, she interpreted it in light of her personal struggle with fear of reading failure. Yet, Arlene's commentaries also reflect the beginning of a change—from being a person who "doesn't find herself doing that" (in the "Learning to drive" tape) to a person who felt she had "made a start" (in the "History of English" one). These tapes, of course, were in addition to other kinds of support in class and ongoing work on various reading strategies. Still, within a few weeks, attitudinal shifts began to clear the way for rapid improvement in reading skills. Particularly salient to a teacher of reading, although unfortunately obscured by the limitations of a written transcription that does not show voice quality and rhythm, was Arlene's improved oral fluency. What was a monotonous drone in earlier readings became lively; her voice took on more English-specific intonation patterns. By the time she read "History of English," she sounded less like a word-caller and more like a person making sense of print, creating the text as she read it.

After a year and a half in basic skills courses, Arlene has moved into more academically challenging classes. She reports that she does "all her work," and other teachers comment on her diligence, while sighing that her requests for "extra work" are scarcely disguised bids for approval.

At one point, I bought her Gary Paulsen's *The Crossing* to read when her father became ill and she had to stay home to care for him. "Shall I do a tape?" she asked, and of course I said yes. She read the following passage on the tape:

> *If he stood long enough and smiled in the shy way, old María would sometimes hand him a tortilla and he could get some beans from the pot if he was lucky. And that would cut away the hunger for a time. Once a drunk soldier had believed in his lint [I played it again and again, but that is what she said] and had give him five American dollars ... he had taken it to the two by four café and bought a chicken and a Pepsi Cola and eaten until nothing but bones remained. ... He could still remember eight years later the taste of grease and garlic on his face.*

The new Arlene had prepared her remarks before she taped them. In her carefully measured reading register, she told why she had selected this part to read aloud:

> *I like this book a lot. It was like a cry for help. The main character Mandy was a young boy who had a lot of hardship. He was a orphan struggling for survival in Juarez, Mexico. It described his will to survive at a young age. He had to be a man at a young age. This book also make me think how many kids are out there like Mandy. We are so busy with our own lives we never take a second thought about what it is like for kids without homes that need help. By telling a hopeful story it made me feel like I was right there.*

This new Arlene talked about main character and plot, picking up hints from the book jacket to shape a succinct summary. Then she ended the tape in a more conversational style:

> *Well, Smokey, thanks for letting me read this book. I really enjoy it and I hope when you listen to this tape you will enjoy it as I enjoy reading this book. I especially like the part about Mandy, how whenever he would get something to eat he had to have him a cold Pepsi to get through the day. Just like us, we have to have that c-o-o-l-d Pepsi.*

Arlene was learning to talk about texts in a way that would be valued in English classes she would take in the future: She was beginning to discuss character, to mention main points of the plot. She was also learning that there are connections between life, books, and the community of readers with whom she shares them. What Arlene, and students like her, select to read often reveals much about how they see themselves. The passage she had selected showed me not how perfectly she had "comprehended" the ideas, but rather reflected her "cry for help"; her hunger for the education that, previously out of reach, had now come closer. As she said of the main character in *The Crossing*, her story seemed to be a "hopeful" one.

For students like Arlene, one can say (with Harste, Woodward, & Burke, 1984) that personal engagement is crucial for success with literacy tasks, and that willingness to be vulnerable is inextricably bound up with engagement. Risk-taking helps the learner break out of safe, predictable patterns, even patterns of failure, and learn new strategies. Risks successfully taken build on each other and permit new risks. It is true that Arlene's earliest "analyses" were idiosyncratic, but as she continued to try new tasks, her interpretations became more "in synch" with what a teacher might expect. Without the opportunity to try first, in her own way, she might not have had the courage to continue and succeed.

Teachers may be concerned that such intimate interactions about students' reading will take up more time than they can spare, but few of my students did more than the required "two minutes of tape-recorded reading six times during the semester." Moreover, reading with students does not last forever. The centrality of the student-teacher bond becomes less as the student-text bond grows. The texts themselves began to teach Arlene. Paulsen's book was one that did; other writings followed. It cannot be denied that this classroom strategy forges a new role between teacher and student, one quite different from that in which the teacher transmits and the student receives an object called "text." Within this new role relation, it is not only the students who must take risks.

When working with reading texts in this manner, teachers must not underestimate how unfamiliar print can be. Some students' home language is not written. These students face learning the language of English and the culture of America in addition to the apparatus of writing and written culture. Others must reorient themselves every time they look at print. Reading from left to right in the English style is not easy for students accustomed to a vertical orientation of text. In terms of sheer hours needed to acquire them, we must not minimize these learnings.

What has always seemed most difficult to new readers is the idea that marks on a page are events, plans of action, or pictures-in-words, all of them waiting to be construed, or realized, by a reader. It cannot be presumed that written language is "message" from "author" to "reader." Myron Tuman (1987, pp. 23-25) has suggested that the distinctive qualities of literacy are represented by this model:

Reader/writer prior to encounter with text _____	text _____	Reader/writer after encounter with text

This model of literacy suggests that reading is essentially a transformative act, that what happens inside the student is what is important. Teachers can assist in a transformative, meaning-making process. The tape-recorded journal allows the teacher to participate in this transformation that learning brings and that brings learning. If teachers continually tell students how meaning is made, guiding them to find only the same meanings they themselves find and no others, we limit the possibilities of literacy to serve personal, transformative functions.

The tape-recorded journal supports the growth of a tentative new reader into a more experienced and confident meaning-maker. It serves students whose home language is not the spoken or written language of the school. It provides teachers with opportunities to offer personalized instruction. And it gives the classroom researcher/teacher an added bonus: The opportunity to learn more about how adults construct meaning from text when school language and written English are acquired late in life.

References

Atwell, N. (1987). *In the middle: Writing, reading, and learning with adolescents.* Upper Montclair, NJ: Boynton/Cook.

Bleich, D. (1989). Reconceiving literacy: Language use and social relations. In C. Anson (Ed.), *Writing and response: Theory, practice, and research.* Urbana, IL: National Council of Teachers of English.

Cook-Gumperz, J. (Ed.). (1986). *The social construction of literacy.* Cambridge: Cambridge University Press.

Graves, D. (1990). *Discovering your own literacy: The reading and writing teachers' companion.* Portsmouth, NH: Heinemann Books.

Harste, J., Woodward, W., & Burke, K. (1984). *Language stories and literacy lessons.* Portsmouth, NH: Heinemann.

Rosen, H. (1971). *Language, the learner, and the school.* London: Penquin Books.

Tuman, M. (1987). *A preface to literacy.* Tuscaloosa, AL:University of Alabama Press.

Walworth, M. (1990). Interactive teaching of reading: A model. In J. K. Peyton (Ed.), *Students and teachers writing together: Perspectives on journal writing* (pp. 37-47). Washington, DC: Teachers of English to Speakers of Other Languages.

6

Dialogue Journal Writing as Part of a Learner-Centered Curriculum

Janet Isserlis
International Institute of Rhode Island
Providence, Rhode Island

That literacy and language exist within a sociocultural context is not a new notion. Countless practitioners and researchers reflect this sociological perspective in literacy studies (e.g., Heath, 1983; Goswami & Stillman, 1987; Scollon & Scollon, 1978). The use of dialogue journal writing in learner-centered ESL literacy classrooms reflects and validates the sociocultural contexts in which adult literacy learners function.

This chapter describes the role of dialogue journal writing within a learner-centered pedagogy, showing how open-ended written dialogue can help to guide the curriculum, address various needs of learners and facilitators in literacy classes, and eventually lead to increased student involvement in shaping their own learning.

From Dialogue to Curricular Themes

Two overriding assumptions shape a learner-centered pedagogy: That literacy exists within a sociocultural context, and that classroom content is driven by learners' needs. In line with these assumptions, classroom organization can be broken down into two broad strands:

recurring events and themes. Recurring events are various types of spontaneous oral or written communication. Students relate ideas or experiences of interest, ask questions of each other, or otherwise interact verbally and communicatively in "classroom news" or language experience activities. Themes and course content often emerge from these interactions.

Dialogue journal writing, as one type of recurring event, can serve as a focal point for a class in a number of ways. Work in dialogue journals provides ongoing reading and writing interaction and allows learners to experience the written word as a communicative form. Journals can generate topics and can give the classroom facilitator a valuable glimpse into adult learners' lives and concerns (the term facilitator is used in place of teachers as it seems helpful, particularly in adult education, to view the teaching role as one of facilitating learning). Learners can choose the extent to which they divulge these concerns, and they can control the information they wish to exchange. From the exchanges grow themes that can be explored further both in the journal and through other means.

One example of a theme emerging from the recurring event of journal writing occurred when one student, "Elizabeth," responded to an entry about the apparent good health of her child. Elizabeth wrote at length about the fact that the child had been born prematurely, which eventually led to discussion in class about health care, prenatal care, and women's issues generally. The discussion also continued in the journal between Elizabeth and the facilitator, as shown in these brief excerpts from that interaction.

> *October 2, 1989*
>
> *...[my son] is better because He take medice. thank for your answer. I and my family are well. And we had a good weekend. thank my Dear teacher. ...*

> *October 23, 1989*
>
> *...How old is [your son] now? Does he sometimes watch TV in English? I think he's lucky, because he is growing up hearing 2 languages--he'll be able to know Spanish and English. Do your other kids speak both languages, too?*

October 23, 1989

...[my son] have 2 1/2 year old. When He Born He weingh 2 Pounds now he have 27 Pounds. he Barn from only sixth month. Some times he watch cartoons But he like played with her toys. He Can said some words in English. Yes my other Kids speak English and Spanish.

October 30, 1989

...and about [son's name]--I'm happy that he's growing up. I didn't know that he was born 3 months early. He's a great kid. Do you think you'll want to have any more children?

October 30, 1989

...I'm very happy too by my son [name] he is very active and entilgent I want more chidren. My husband want a girls. But the Doctor's say I can have not more beacause is danger for me. But anyway I want more children.

November 16, 1989

[In response to my questions about the possible danger of having more children]

...the Doctor say is dangerous By my Hight Pleasurre. [highblood pressure] Now I have another Doctor is a woman Doctor But she is very nice.

The point here is that a curriculum topic cannot be imposed upon a group of learners but may emerge through the journal exchange and other ongoing discussions and literacy activities. The learners in the situation described here addressed the issue of health care after the student herself introduced the topic first in the journal and then in the group.

When identifying themes, facilitators need to be sensitive to students' privacy. If a common theme such as health care seems to be emerging in the journals, the facilitator might privately ask each learner if that theme can be explored with others in the class.

Demystifying Writing

Second language learners tend to resist writing, but interaction in the dialogue journal can help to demystify the process. By encouraging small increments of reading and writing to occur within each session, the facilitator helps learners to become engaged in the process slowly. After three or four journal exchanges, learners generally increase the amount of writing they do, and often their understanding of the facilitator's entries increases as well.

Initially, beginning literacy students may be able to answer basic questions such as "How are you today?" or "Where do you live?" As time goes on, the repetition of such "How are you? How do you feel?" questions provides a predictable format through which more independent reading and writing skills gradually develop. Francine Filipek Collignon, with the literacy ESL program at the International Institute of Rhode Island, also suggests the use of photo albums in which learners collect images of significance and label and codify them in a way that has meaning to them, as a means of moving them toward the written journal form. Learners gradually do learn to read and write. One man's description of a photo of himself taken during class, written after two months of weekly dialogue journal writing, indicates an awareness of his own progress with writing:

> I am Joe and in the picture I was writing a letter abouth my family. Now I have lost my fear to write because when the classes began two months ago I was afraid of writing.

Integrating Volunteers

The journal provides a means for integrating volunteer tutors (or new facilitators) into the classroom. Learners who lack the skills needed to read the facilitator's entries independently or to generate their own responses may wish to dictate those responses to the tutor. The tutor also has an opportunity to observe learners during this process and to learn about their interactions with literacy and with each other. This integration of the tutor within the classroom enhances learners' feelings about being tutored. The "pull-out" model can be stigmatizing to some learners. Instead, having someone in class who works with many learners but who may focus on one or two, is less observably a form of "special help" or worse, "remediation."

Promoting Interaction Among Learners

In the absence of a tutor, or when one facilitator cannot be available to all learners, a learner can also turn to a more experienced co-learner. Although the primary intent of the journal may be a one-to-one communication between learner and facilitator, learners rarely hesitate to seek assistance from each other when they are engaged in responding to a journal entry. The journals provide genuine reasons for working for and with each other—more able readers and writers help the less advanced.

Providing Classroom Structure

Dialogue journals can also provide a sense of structure to the ESL literacy classroom. Students frequently state that they want structure, and often this means grammar lessons or workbooks. In a truly learner-centered classroom, concerns such as these are of paramount importance. Facilitators need to respect students' perceptions of what learning is, while considering the implication (and limitations) of the actual learning that may occur within the textbook or worksheet construct. It does little good to tell learners that, although they may score perfectly on a worksheet involving the past tense, they will frequently still report that "Yesterday I go to downtown."

Learners and facilitators can strike a compromise. Structure can evolve from the seemingly loose construct of the dialogue journal. First, maintaining a regular writing time provides a formal structure to the class. Second, in reading the journals, facilitators learn about frequently made errors. They may take note of individual students' problem areas and address them separately within the journal or in class.

Facilitators may notice, for example, that the use of -ed for the past tense is problematic for many learners, and so develop exercises or lessons around that particular construction. In working out ways to individualize student work, reading and writing problems that surface in the journal may suggest activities for individual or small group work.

Demonstrating Progress

Once students become accustomed to the regularity of journal writing, they are eager to initiate newcomers to the process. "Veteran" students help newcomers, frequently explaining in the native language what the process is and how to get started. As time passes, learners may see for themselves the extent to which their writing has developed in length and quality. The facilitator may already know that learners are making progress with literacy; the dialogue journal helps learners to see that progress for themselves.

Promoting Student Independence

An important goal of adult literacy programs is that learners become independent, determining the direction of their learning and taking responsibility for it. Dialogue journal writing is one way to promote that independence. For example, the adult students in the literacy ESL program at the International Institute of Rhode Island, given the option of continuing classes once weekly during a summer break (after a regular schedule of four nights per week), agreed to that schedule, but requested additional study time as well. Their facilitators were unable to meet with them a second night, but presented them the option of meeting independently to work on dialogue journals and generate a classroom newspaper. These activities had been modeled throughout the regular school year, so students were quite familiar with the process and methodologies involved. About three quarters of the original student body returned for this independent study one day each week. Some took on the facilitator's role of helping others read entries in the journals and write responses. Learners demonstrated through their ongoing attendance and participation that they were capable of expanding and developing the learning community that had been built during the year and of implementing the methodologies they had learned.

Conclusions

Written interaction in dialogue journals can provide the basis for a variety of literacy events and activities within a learner-centered second language classroom at any level. Such interaction can be sustained over extended periods, making the use of dialogue journals adaptable and flexible to virtually all teaching and learning situations. The journal is one vehicle through which learners can express their concerns and interests. Learners who wish to have a place to express deeply personal issues and others choosing to reveal less of themselves still have an opportunity to engage in writing. As learners reveal concerns and needs in their writing, themes, questions, and answers are generated. The attentive facilitator learns to follow up in appropriate ways on these areas of concern. Gradually students become more independent and assertive and begin to make their own decisions about the forms and directions their learning might take.

References

Goswami, D., & Stillman, P. (Eds.). (1987). *Reclaiming the classroom.* Portsmouth, NH: Heinemann.

Heath, S. B. (1983). *Ways with words.* Cambridge: Cambridge University.

Scollon, R., & Scollon, S. (1978). *Narrative, literacy, and face in interethnic communication.* Norwood, NJ: Ablex.

7

Dialogue Journal Writing with a Language Associate to Learn a Foreign Language

Diane Poole
Summer Institute of Linguistics
Tucson, Arizona

Diane Poole and her colleague, Judi Lynn Anderson, are linguists working with the Summer Institute of Linguistics (SIL) in Tucson, Arizona. They work closely with a "language associate," a native speaker of Chinantec, a language spoken in Oaxaca, Mexico, to learn to speak Chinantec, develop written texts in Chinantec, and translate the Bible into Chinantec. Much of their work has been done in their associate's village, Comaltepec. Because they are currently able to work there only infrequently, the language associate goes to Tucson to work with them.

When I read about the use of dialogue journal writing for promoting language acquisition and literacy (Peyton, 1986), I decided that it was an excellent approach for my co-worker, Judi Lynn Anderson, and I to use with our language associate (LA), a native Chinantec speaker. Although we had acquired considerable oral proficiency in Chinantec, we needed to improve our written proficiency. We also wanted our LA to grow in his ability to express himself naturally and fluently by writing in his own language. Because he spends several months at a time working with us in Tucson, where the Mexico branch of SIL is currently located, he is away from his village where he is immersed in his language. Therefore, he tends to lose the sharp edge of naturalness and begins to adapt his speech to our far-from-natural style.

Our experiment with dialogue journal writing in the native language of our LA lasted over a five-week period during one of his stays in Tucson. At the start of each day's work, each of us wrote in our journals for about half an hour or less, about any topic we chose, in Chinantec. Then we came together and read our entries aloud to one another. Our LA read his first, and we made comments about the topic or asked questions about the meanings of words and how these words were used in various contexts. Then we read aloud what we had written. Our LA, now in the role of teacher, asked us questions, usually for clarification because our errors made the meaning unclear. He then corrected our writing, reading, or pronunciation. Topics included our first trip to our LA's village, our appreciation that our LA had come to join us in Tucson to continue working with us, his journey out of the village to travel to the United States, and fiestas in his village. We also wrote about difficulties we were all having adjusting to life in Tucson. The English translation of a portion of an entry written in Chinantec by Judi Lynn and the translation of an entry written by our LA appear below.

October 29, 1986

Judi Lynn

During the night our dog, Rufus, barked. I don't know why. And the coyotes were howling in the mountains. I like it when they howl. And when it got light Rufus barked again.

LA

Now in Comaltepec the fiesta of Mii Madsee is approaching on November 20th. And many people go to that fiesta and take the opportunity to pick oranges because it is the season for them. And the young men also go to play basketball because there is a tournament, and many people from other

53

places also go to play. And sometimes they give excellent prizes for the first three places. They have given a bull or a pig or a turkey. So many people get excited about going and think how they can win. And if there are many teams, they play only for two days, and if only a few [teams] then only for a day and a half.

In deciding to use journal writing with our LA, we were facing a different situation than that experienced by teachers in the United States teaching English as a second language. Whereas those teachers write in their native language while their students write in their second or third language, here our LA was writing in his native language. All three of us, therefore, became learners in a sense, working at different levels. We linguists were learning to speak and write in our second or third language. Our LA, who was in fact the "teacher" in this situation, was also improving his ability to write in his mother tongue.

We gained a number of benefits from this experience. With the daily practice of writing freely in his own language, our LA gained greater fluency and naturalness in writing, even though he had been writing in his own language for several years. When he was away from his home environment for long periods to work with us, he had no opportunity to use his language with anyone except us, and our proficiency was very limited. The routine of daily journal writing gave him the rare opportunity for extended natural use of his language. As a result, his translation of the texts we were working on improved. He was also affirmed as a speaker and writer of his mother tongue, because what he wrote was important enough for us to ask questions about and express interest in.

By writing daily in Chinantec and having our LA ask questions about and comment on our journal entries, we learned a tremendous amount about Chinantec and improved our control of it in both speaking and writing. Our incorrect language use and thought processes became apparent and were slowly replaced with correct expressions and ideas. When we found, through our oral reading of our entries and discussions of them, that we did not control an aspect of the language, we focused on that area in our subsequent writing and in our daily language use.

We found that the quality of our relationship with our LA also improved. He was able to express some of his feelings without fear or embarrassment, because we had developed a relationship of trust.

54

Possibly because of the journal writing, he shared with us some of his struggles for the first time in the four years we had been working with him. I personally was able to share more feelings and concerns in my journal writings than I had done before, and I found that this seemed to help our LA to do the same. For example, after I had written about the culture stress I experienced living in Tucson (I am from England), he shared some of the culture stress he was experiencing; he expressed some homesickness when he wrote at length and in some detail about current village events, and bewilderment about never knowing what language he would be addressed in while living in Tucson—English, Spanish, or his own. Because of the journal writing, we were all willing to share with one another in an atmosphere of interest and acceptance, and the quality of our relationship deepened.

I highly recommend journal writing as an effective tool for developing language and literacy skills, both for linguists learning a language and for the native speakers of that language. Linguists working with a LA can write in a dialogue journal as soon as a writing system is developed for the language, whether they are in the beginning stages or honing more advanced language abilities. The journal writing can also serve to increase the naturalness and fluency of the LA's writing skills, so that his or her translation into the language is more natural. Any opportunity that an LA has to write freely and regularly is going to lead to more natural written language use. Journal writing and sharing allow writing to occur in the context of a relationship rather than in isolation. It is also beneficial for building a relationship between the LA and the linguist and, if done with the right atmosphere, can lead to a level of sharing between two parties that might not otherwise be reached.

Note

This article is reprinted, with permission, from *Dialogue*, 5(1), April, 1988.

Reference

Peyton, J.K. (1986).Literacy through written interaction. *Passage: A Journal for Refugee Education*, 2(1), 24-29.

8

Dialogue Journal Entries as Problem-Posing Codes

Laura Klos Sokol
Georgetown University
Washington, DC

The problem-posing approach to second language teaching, used with adult learners in ESL classes at the Spanish Education Development (SED) Center in Washington, DC, is inspired by the work of Brazilian educator Paulo Freire. Freire, who believes that education should be participatory and liberating, advocates discussing social problems in the classroom, with the goal of helping learners to think critically about situations in their own lives (cf. Spener, 1990). Freire believes that dialogue is central to the learning process, for "true dialogue cannot exist unless it involves critical thinking, thinking which sees reality as a process, in transformation, thinking which does not separate itself from action but constantly involves itself in the real struggle without fear of the risks involved" (Freire, 1970, p. 62).

Problem-posing activities are one approach advocated by Freire to elicit such meaningful dialogue among adult learners. These activities revolve around the use of "codes"—problem situations that are directly relevant to the learners' lives. A code can take the form of a dialogue, a story, a picture, or whatever the instructor chooses, as long as the problem presented in the code is familiar to the participants. The use of codes provides a curriculum based on material from the students' own lives, enabling them to react to and analyze issues that are relevant to them. The codes often elicit strong feelings, and students are less inclined to focus on language form because they are intent on getting an important message across. Students are put in a position of control, as they identify courses of action that may offer solutions to the problem. It is important to distinguish between problem-*posing* and problem-*solving* activities. In problem-solving approaches, educators identify problems for the students a priori, and then design lessons to give them the knowledge or skills they need to solve those problems. In problem-posing approaches, students identify problems and their possible causes and propose actions that might be taken to solve them. The problem and its solutions come from the group (cf. Spener, 1990, for discussion).

There are five basic steps students use for responding to a code (cf. Wallerstein, 1983).

1. Describe the code presented (e.g., What is happening?).
2. Identify the specific problem involved.
3. Discuss whether the problem presented is relevant to students' or their friends' lives, and express any feelings they might have about the conflict.
4. Identify the possible causes of the problem.
5. Suggest any individual or group actions that might alleviate the problem.

Rather than talking through all of the steps, it is better to vary them with activities such as role-playing, written compositions, and discussions in small groups.

The SED Center curriculum provides a multitude of prepared codes related to male and female roles, daily routines, health, and immigration, but the instructors are encouraged to create suitable codes as well. Dialogue journals can be an ideal source for codes, because the context often revolves around important issues in students' lives.

During one six-week session, I used entries from my students' dialogue journals as codes for class discussion. I obtained the students' permission before using any dialogue journal entry in class and promised complete confidentiality. To avoid any kind of embarrassment on the student's part, I sometimes changed specific information in the entry that could possibly reveal the writer's identity, or concocted a related situation based on a student entry. This way, the code was still based on the original entry, but the student's identity was well protected.

The following is an example of a dialogue journal entry used in my class as a problem-posing code.

> *I think confusion in my life. Sometime I'm very very boring. I think a live alon all the time. My husband not have time for me. He is only think and work in your life I have different idea because he is too much in years too me.*

Everyone was given a copy of the entry, and we corrected it on the board, identifying specific errors in grammar, spelling, and punctuation. We then divided into two discussion groups for the first three steps of problem posing. The situation seemed to be a familiar one to most of the students, and several interpretations of the problem were suggested. Both men and women discussed experiences that they described as characterized by "domineering Hispanic husbands." For the fourth step, the students wrote individual essays speculating on the cause of the problem, and then came back together for a class discussion of what they had written. The fifth step involved proposing and evaluating solutions to the problem in groups. Suggested solutions ranged from getting a divorce to having a baby, but almost everyone finally agreed that the couple needed to improve their communication by discussing the problem outright.

My six-week experience with using selected dialogue journal texts for problem-posing activities indicated to me that they can be an excellent source for codes that come directly from the learners' lives. For anyone else wishing to do the same, a few points should be kept in mind. First, a code chosen from a dialogue journal should represent a situation that could be relevant to everyone in the class, and not simply to a specific student; otherwise, class discussion can turn into a group therapy session. The problem should be focused on one conflict, since several conflicts presented in one situation can be overwhelming.

Second, the instructor must decide if an entry will be used as a code in the class of the person who wrote it. If students realize that their writing might be used for class discussion, they may become inhibited about writing in their journals. On the other hand, if a class is very close and students are open, they sometimes enjoy discussing their journal writing with each other. Whether or not the codes come from the writing of students in a given class, their permission must be obtained and their identities strictly protected.

One problem that I encountered was finding enough suitable dialogue journal entries for class use. Building a collection of entries over time from several classes solves this problem and eliminates the risk of embarrassing students by using their entries when they are present in class.

Dialogue journal entries provide real-life data for problem-posing codes, and therefore can be one means to fulfilling Freire's stated purpose of education: To liberate people, by allowing them to discuss problems that are relevant to them and helping them to realize that they are sources of creative, critical thinking and capable of action in the face of conflict.

Note

This article is reprinted, with permission, from *Dialogue*, 5(1), April, 1988.

References

Freire, P. (1970). *Pedagogy of the oppressed*. New York: The Continuum Publishing Corporation.

Spener, D. (1990). *The Freirian Approach to Adult Literacy Education*. Washington, DC: National Clearinghouse on Literacy Education.

Wallerstein, N. (1983). *Language and culture in conflict*. Reading, MA: Addison-Wesley.

9

Full Cycle: From Journal Writing to "Codes" to Writing

Loren McGrail
Adult Literacy Resource Institute
Roxbury Community College
Boston, Massachusetts

> *My husdpan speak to me in English. And I understand*
> *everything he said to me . But I didn't speak to him in*
> *English because I don't want he see my mistake. Because I*
> *embaresse in front of him. He speak to me in English and*
> *I speak to him in Spanish. only i speak in English with my*
> *auughter and the people in the street. I go to the hospital*
> *and when I go to my daughter's school because her teacher*
> *speak in English.*

The above journal entry comes from Carmen, a student in a family literacy class at El Centro del Cardenal in Boston, Massachusetts. At the end of every week, for about 10 to 15 minutes, we wrote in our journals. We wrote at the end of the week and not at the beginning for three reasons. The first was to avoid students' tendency to focus on what they had done over the weekend, and instead, to encourage students to talk about what they were learning. Second, those students who didn't finish or who wanted to write more could take their journals home. Finally, I had a little more time to respond over the weekend.

Carmen's entry came in response to a series of questions from me about her daughter. When I read this entry I found it provocative and rich in detail. Why did she feel embarrassed to speak English with her husband? Why was he speaking in English to her in the first place? Why was she more comfortable with her daughter or people in the street? The entry also reminded me of the ways we can all be perceived as being like her husband; the ways we can unknowingly censor someone or inhibit them from expressing themselves. I have often felt like this husband in my own classroom, speaking English knowing that students understand me but will not speak back.

When I wrote back to Carmen, I asked her if she would share her writing with the class because I felt others might have had similar experiences. I thought we could talk about it as a group to see if, collectively, we could come up with possible strategies for dealing with these feelings of embarrassment. I also wanted to see if we could come up with some strategies to increase the positive moments as well. Carmen was open to sharing her writing and comfortable with letting the class know she was the author, with the condition that I proof it for spelling and grammar errors.

Carmen's writing struck me as being a perfect "code," to use Freirean terms. It was a problem situation that was relevant to others (Laura Klos Sokol also describes the use of dialogue journal entries as "codes" in her article in this volume). The situation was also open enough that people could interpret it in many different ways. For example, this class focused its discussion on what it was like for them to go back to school and take ESL, and how this was changing their roles in the home. Another class focused on the husband. Some of the women felt he was being macho and intimidating their classmate, while others argued that he might be a North American or Puerto Rican who is English dominant. Both classes were given the code and questions below.

> *My husband speaks to me in English. And I understand everything he says to me but I don't speak to him in English because I don't want to make mistakes because I am embarrassed in front of him. He speaks to me in English and I speak to him in Spanish. Only I speak in English to my daughter and the people in the street or when I go to the hospital or my daughter's school because her teacher speaks English.*

Questions:
1. Is the writer a man or a woman?
   What language does she use to speak to her husband?
   What language does she use to speak to her daughter?
   Which other people does she speak English with? Why?
   Why does she speak English when she goes to her daughter's school?

2. Why does her husband speak English to her?
   Why does she speak Spanish to him?
   Why is she embarrassed?
   Why does she speak English to her daughter?

3. Have you ever felt embarrassed about speaking English? Describe what happened.
   How do you think her daughter feels? Do you have children?
   How do you feel speaking English with them?
   How do you think her husband feels? Have you ever felt like him before?

4. When are you most comfortable speaking English? Why?
   When are you least comfortable speaking English? Why?
   What can you do to feel more comfortable about speaking English?
   What is your native tongue? When do you speak it and with whom?

Follow-up activities:
Write in the voice of the husband or the daughter about how you think they might feel.
Write a dialogue between the husband and the wife using two languages.

In both classes the students did not want to do my suggested follow-up activities. They wanted to write instead about their own linguistic situation at home—who was speaking which language to whom. The code thus acted as a prewriting activity that stimulated more writing.

During the middle of the writing and rewriting, we still carried on our regular journal writing. One day in one of my student's journals I noticed some writing that clearly was not done by her. It turned out that the writing was done by her daughter. I suggested that if the daughter wanted to correspond with me, I would be happy to give the student another journal to give to her daughter so that she, too, could write to me. About a week later I received an entry from her daughter. The following is an excerpt from her daughter's journal:

> *I'm glad my mother is going to school so she could speak English. It finally mean that I don't have to translate for her ...it must be hard for you to teach the students. You'll also got to be patient. I really can't do that. I'll never be a good teacher because I am not good at teaching.*

The daughter's entry about her relief at being able to give up her role as translator added another dimension to the issue of which language(s) one should use, when, and why. When I shared the daughter's writing with the class (again with permission), it brought up a whole new related issue—bilingual education. This became the seed for another cycle of literacy activities. It also helped to inspire some students to write more candidly about how their children feel toward their parents learning English or going to school. We decided to put these writings together and make a small self-published book that was circulated among class members.

At the end of this process, I discovered that we had moved quite naturally from private to public writing, from journals to shared stories. The single voice, the individual issue, had become a collective voice identifying and refining issues that were important to many.

Note

A similar version of this article appears in a book chapter co-authored with Elsa Auerbach, "Rosa's challenge: Connecting classroom and community contexts," to be published in Sarah Benesch (Ed.), *ESL in America: Myths and possibilities in linguistic minority education*, Boynton/ Cook Publishers.

Dear Caty
I'm glad after you know
I sty verry happy with you. because
is a good teacher. you live in
washington. with your husbands.
sood.
I'm live in washington too
because in my country I have much
problems now.
Thank you Caty
     Sincerely
         Marija

Dear Maruja,
I am sorry about the problems in
Peru.
   this weekend I am going to the state
of North Carolina. My husband's cousin
is getting married and we are going
to drive to the wedding
We will come back on Sunday
       Sincerely
        Cathy

Part III

Working with Beginning Writers

Literacy educators are concerned most about those adult students who have received little or no schooling in their first language and now must master both literacy and a second language at the same time. To address these real concerns, this section focuses on the needs and potential of the very beginning writer using dialogue journals.

This section highlights the major differences for the beginning adult writer between spoken and written communication, and points out the value for these students of beginning with a hybrid form of communication like dialogue journals. Dialogue journal conversations share valuable characteristics of oral conversation—especially the support of turn-taking with a known audience who responds to each comment, and equally valuable aspects of written language—time for reflection, lack of interruptions, and the greater demand for explicitness or elaboration of thoughts in order to communicate clearly. We have often called dialogue journals a bridge from oral to written communication. In working with very beginning limited literacy students, they are indeed a valuable bridge.

David Spener draws on his experience working in an innovative home-based program, Inglés en Su Casa, to describe the value, but also the difficulties, of initiating dialogue journals with such students. Studies of development over time in the dialogue journals of beginning adult literacy students still need to be done. Julietta Davis makes a first attempt, in her study of the painstaking growth of one beginning writer in the surface forms of her writing, and in the metacognitions concerning what acquiring those forms means. Her findings demonstrate clearly that the lack of mastery of surface forms does not inhibit the ability to communicate meaningful messages in writing, and that mastery develops as the practice of meaningful written communication continues.

10

Getting Started: Dialogue Journal Writing with Semiliterate Adult ESL Students

David Spener
National Clearinghouse on Literacy Education
Center for Applied Linguistics
Washington, DC

I have taught beginning ESL to adult students for a number of years and in a variety of settings. In most classes, I have used dialogue journals as a tool to help my students develop their writing skills during the earliest stages of their learning of English. Many of the students I have worked with were semiliterate in their native language, and for some, the dialogue journal was their first experience with prose writing since childhood. I found dialogue journals to be helpful not only as a vehicle for communicative writing practice for my students, but also as a vital source of information for me about their lives and cultures. Using dialogue journals effectively, however, did not come immediately or automatically. Through a process of trial and error, I eventually developed a practice that was gratifying to me and my students, and one that seemed to further their literacy development. For the benefit of other teachers contemplating using dialogue journals with ESL literacy students, I relate some of my experiences here.

A First Attempt

My first experience with dialogue journals was as a very new teacher at the Spanish Education Development (SED) Center in Washington, DC. I had volunteered at SED and gotten my first exposure to dialogue journals from my mentor teacher, Julietta Hester (now Davis), who used them regularly in her classes. My first assignment as a paid teacher there was with the "low-level I class," composed mainly of Central American students who had received less than a second-grade education in their home country. No one in class was completely illiterate: everyone could write their name, knew the alphabet, and could write simple sentences in Spanish, albeit with a great deal of labor and with childlike script. Most spoke and understood only a few words of English. I was inexperienced at using dialogue journals with students, but went ahead anyway, mostly on faith: I had been told that they were a good, communicative, nonintimidating way to get students to practice writing, and I was interested in "dialoguing" with my students at every possible opportunity.

At SED, teachers were given blank blue university exam books for student dialogue journals. At first I thought these books would be very intimidating to the students, but then realized that they had never seen blue exam books before and did not share the sense of collegiate dread that they provoked in me. After we had been in class together for a few weeks, I decided to introduce the dialogue journals at the end of class one night. I handed out the blue books and asked the students to write their name on the cover. While they wrote their names, I wrote my first "letter" to them on the blackboard:

February 8, 1985

Dear Class,

How are you tonight? This is my first letter to you. I'm from Missouri. My parents live in Missouri. My father is a salesman. My mother works in an office. Tell me something about your family.

Your teacher,

David

After I explained that we were going to use the books for sending letters back and forth between them and me, I read my letter orally, reviewing its structure and suggesting ways they could answer it. Then, I asked them to respond to it by writing a letter back to me in their books. (I did this all in English.) With about 15 minutes left in class, I strolled around the room, looking over students' shoulders and answering their questions about the task. Hands were shooting up everywhere, and it was evident that many of my students had not understood quite what they were supposed to be doing. When I collected the journals and the students had left for the evening, I quickly leafed through their responses to my letter. A few students, the more advanced and those that I had helped, responded "appropriately" by writing the date, "Dear David," giving the information I had asked for, and closing with "Your student." Others were headed in that direction, but had not had time to finish their letter, stopping in midword. Several students simply wrote their name on the page. A substantial percentage of the class copied my letter into their journals. Some simply copied sentences they had written previously in class that had nothing to do with answering my letter. (For example, "Dear Class, mi NAme Jose. I from Salbador.") A couple of students wrote nothing at all. I thought I had given clear, easy-to-follow instructions, but clearly many either had not understood what to do or were unable to do it.

At home between classes, I wrote individual letters back to students trying to respond to what, if anything, they had written. To those who had written something, but had not responded to what my letter asked for, I wrote things like the following:

February 12, 1985

Dear José,

Thanks for your letter. Please answer this question: What part of El Salvador are you from? Please tell me something about your FAMILY. I have 1 sister. She goes to school in Connecticut...

I did not correct any errors in grammar, spelling, or vocabulary. When I handed the blue books back to students the next class period, I again explained what I had done in their books and what I wanted them to do, this time in Spanish, hoping to eliminate any confusion left over from the last class. This time the results were better—more students responded "appropriately" to my letters and some even asked me some questions. A few, the least literate and least proficient in oral English, still copied my letter, wrote down unrelated sentences that they had memorized, or wrote nothing.

As the eight-week course progressed, I continued to initiate dialogue with students in their blue books by asking them questions that I hoped they knew how to answer because we had already covered similar material in class. This gave the ones who were able to respond and exchange information some additional practice at reading and writing the things they were beginning to learn to say and understand in class. I would not say, however, that we really had much of a dialogue going— the information shared was mostly contrived and predictable, and was related to the grammar and survival competencies of the rest of the ESL curriculum. And, in fact, I was always the one initiating the exchange. Students seemed to respond to the extent to which they were a) interested in practicing their writing, b) interested in pleasing the teacher, and c) developmentally able.

Some students in the course never got beyond copying my letter or writing their name or some memorized sentences. At least, I rationalized, they were practicing the act of writing, and if that was all they were able to do or interested in doing at this point, then they could just as well do it in their dialogue journals as anyplace else. There was no embarrassment for them in this, either. Dialogue journals were a private, uncensored and uncensured thing between each student and me. No one else knew what they were writing. When the course ended, they were able to keep their journals, either for posterity or for use in their next course.

What had I accomplished by using dialogue journals in this way? I felt it hadn't generated really meaningful dialogue. It had given some of the students their first opportunity to exchange information in written English and also helped reinforce the vocabulary and structures we were studying in class, but another kind of activity might have better served that purpose.

Some students never did more than rote copying in their books, and that only when pressed to do so. A couple of years later, I bumped into one of these students, a Guatemalan woman in her fifties, at a party at the home of a friend of her daughter. She told me (in much better English than I had ever heard her speak before) that she had progressed on to the more advanced levels of the ESL program before taking some time off from studying, but that she still had copies of her first blue book dialogue journals and intended to keep them as a record of where she had started. This made me wonder if the most important function of dialogue journals in that first class had been historical and not educational, as a record of the passage from the mother country to the new country, to be found in an old chest years later by some inquisitive grandchildren.

A More Successful Beginning

Several years after this first experience, I found myself teaching small groups of Spanish-speaking students in their own homes as part of the SED Center's family literacy program, Inglés en Su Casa. I was following a bilingual approach to literacy development in my classes, attempting to build students' conceptual knowledge of language first in Spanish and subsequently in English. The small size of the classes (five to ten people), the existence of teacher-student dialogue in Spanish and English from the first day of class, and my own higher level of experience as a teacher and user of dialogue journals smoothed the introduction to dialogue journals. These classes were multilevel in oral English proficiency and native language literacy, and I thought that dialogue journal writing would help give each student the particular kind of practice needed to progress.

We discussed the purpose of the journals before I handed them out to each student with an individual letter already written on the first page. Before I had them begin to write their letters back to me, I modeled on newsprint writing the date, salutation, and closure of an English letter.

In my first letter, I attempted to tailor the level of reading difficulty to each student's particular level. When I knew that a student understood no English whatsoever, I wrote the body of my letter in Spanish, with the date, salutation, and closure in English. I included questions in the text of my letter that I thought would engage the particular student I was writing to, basing these educated guesses on information I'd received from previous conversations with that student or with others. In these small groups in people's homes, I had the advantage of operating with much more intimate knowledge of my students than in my earlier experiences using dialogue journals.

I encouraged students in these classes to write as much in English as possible in their journals, but to go ahead and inject a word or phrase in Spanish if they didn't know how to say something in English. Some were reluctant to write in English at first, even though they had demonstrated their ability to do so in other class activities. After receiving a few total-Spanish letters responding to my English letters, I asked them pointedly in a letter to start writing to me in English. (These were English classes, after all!) Some students' journals showed a progression from extensive use of Spanish to extensive use of English over the course of several months.

In these home-based classes, I had several students who were nearly illiterate in Spanish. They could not manage a pencil very well, and had difficulty forming the letters of the alphabet. I tried several ways of facilitating their participation in journal writing. One strategy I used was to give these students two blue books. During class, when everyone else was responding to my letters, I worked with them on copying exercises in one of their blue books. I wrote my letters to them, in Spanish, in the other book. Rather than have them attempt to write back, I would ask them if they had a friend or someone in their family who could read and write in Spanish. If the answer was yes (and it usually was), I asked them to have that friend read them my letter and to write down their dictated response to me in their blue book, also in Spanish. Although some of these students produced a few letters back to me, follow-through outside of class for this assignment was generally low. Looking back on it now, I think that giving minimally literate students an assignment where they are dependent on a literate person for its completion may in fact heighten the dependence they suffer already as a result of their illiteracy. It seems to me in hindsight that one cannot help others become more independent by having them practice dependent behaviors.

One particularly poignant example of the failure of this approach was a woman who asked her husband, also a member of the class, to write her dictated letters to me. Or rather, I suggested that she ask him, and she complied. She never produced a single letter, and shortly afterwards her husband dropped out of the class. It turns out they were in the process of splitting up, in part because the husband didn't want her to learn English, or to read or write Spanish. The fact that she was writing and receiving letters from another man (me) did not sit particularly well with him either, even if the purpose was educational and he was to be an integral part of writing her response.

A more successful approach was to ask the minimally literate students questions that could be answered with pictures. For example, a student could respond to my request to "tell me about your family" with a drawing of family members, perhaps with their ages written next to each one. This gave students more physical practice with a pencil, got them used to expressing ideas with graphic symbols, and engaged them in the same activity as the rest of the class—two-way graphic communication.

Finally, I gave some very beginning writers a broken-line journal entry to trace over (Figure 1). After my letter to them (below), I gave them a template with the date, "Dear David," a response to my question with a blank to fill in, and the closing.

> *March 1, 1988*
>
> *Dear José,*
>
> *Dígame. Dónde vive tu familia? Mi familia vive en San Luis de Missouri.*
>
> *Sincerely,*
>
> *David*

Typically, I or another student would sit with the student, read my letter word-by-word with him aloud, read him the response, and ask him to fill in any blanks orally. Then, either the helping student or I would fill in the blanks with broken-line letters for him to trace over. This strategy was perhaps the most socially inclusive for the least literate students in a given class. It, too, required dependence either upon me or another, more literate student, but I felt that at least it went beyond mere copying exercises or having somebody else write for them.

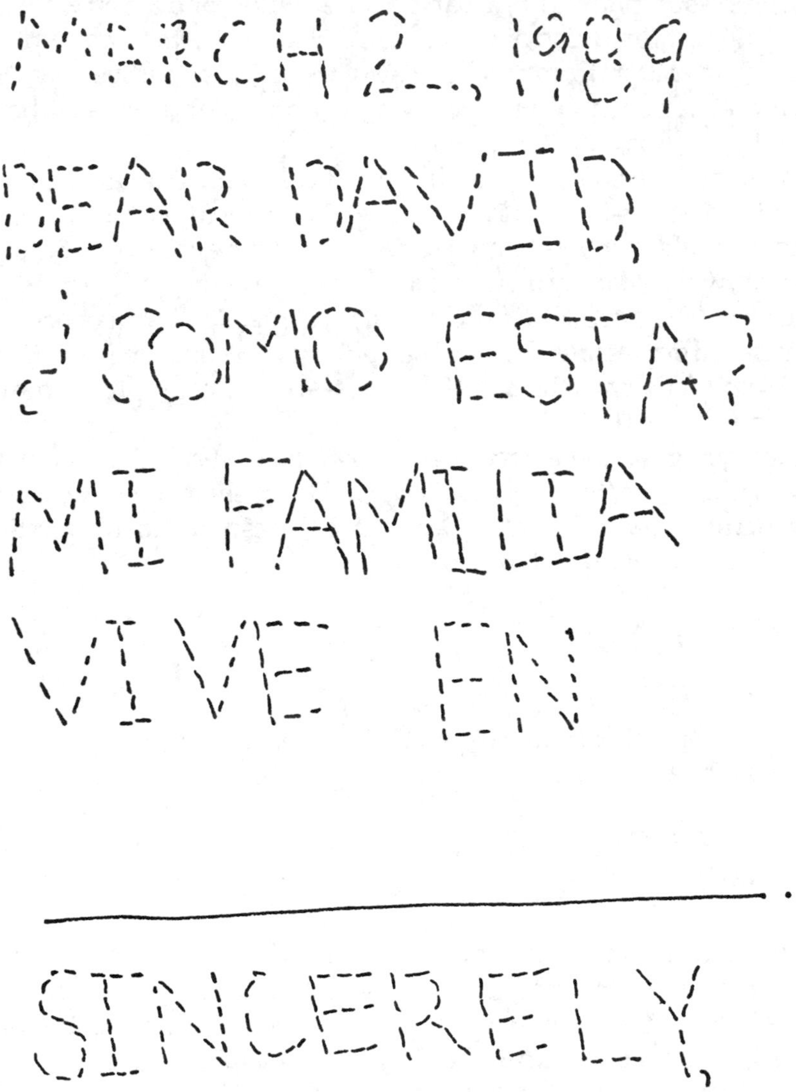

MARCH 2, 1989

DEAR DAVID,

¿COMO ESTA?

MI FAMILIA

VIVE EN

_____ .

SINCERELY,

Figure 1. Broken-line journal entry used with
minimally literate students.

Tracing over broken lines is like painting by numbers in that the only thing the person painting by numbers can creatively add to the picture is the color of her or his choosing. My new-writer students could add their one-word responses to my questions, and not much else. Whether or not painting by numbers helps a person learn how to paint is the kind of question that could also be asked regarding new writers in this situation. With mixed results, I tried to wean these individuals gradually from the "boiler-plate" format by removing nonvariant parts, such as the salutation and the closing, and by encouraging them to write a question for me to answer after filling in their boiler-plate response. Here, I encountered another problem, which was that the 10 to 15 minutes I gave students to write in their journals was not usually enough time for the neoliterates in class to extend their responses beyond what I gave them to trace over and fill in. Krashen (1982) has said that oral language acquisition is triggered by comprehensible input that is at a level slightly above what the language learner can already produce. For the acquisition of literacy in dialogue journals, I would add the crucial element of sufficient time to process the input and organize and produce the output. Putting too much time pressure on students struggling to make sense of what they are reading and to write a cogent response can defeat the purpose of dialogue journals by making them seem like a test.

The letters written to me in the dialogue journals by students in Inglés en Su Casa were typically short, given the amount of time they had in class to read my letter and write a response. Reading their letters at home between classes, I would make a mental note of any significant errors that affected my comprehension as well as those that could easily be modeled correctly. Below the signature on the student letter, and before beginning to write my reply, I would write the word, phrase, or sentence as I might say or write it as a native speaker. Since students' letters were short, they could easily compare what they had written with what a literate native speaker of English would write. When someone wrote all or part of a letter to me in Spanish, I would pick a word or phrase that could be translated easily and modeled in English and copy the original phrase and its translation at the bottom of the student's letter.

In writing my response to student letters, I would repeat things they had said to me, implicitly correcting errors, asking a follow-up question or two, and sharing similar information from my own experience. For example, if a student wrote to me, "I worker construction for 5 yirs," I might write back, "I remember that you are a construction worker. Where are you working now? What construction site? I see they are building (construyendo) many new offices and houses in Washington now...." Through implicit correction of student errors, modeling of native-speaker writing, and engaging students in real-life written communicative situations where information was exchanged and meaning was negotiated, I hoped that students would gradually accommodate their writing toward the native-speaker model in their journal entries.

Over time, I did see definite improvements in my students' dialogue journal writing. Although there is no way of telling whether their gains were due more to explicit instruction in class or implicit learning from the dialogue journals, I feel that students did in fact learn new vocabulary, master some new structures, improve their spelling, and learn to express themselves better as a result of the written dialogue we carried on in their exam books. In some cases, I saw students go from writing almost entirely in Spanish to using English exclusively in their letters to me. Others went from writing a few hesitant lines in each letter to letters of more than two pages in the 15 minutes or so they had to write. Some students began to write more intimate, personal things in their letters to me, sharing some problem they were having or communicating some closely held plan or aspiration.

I wish I had a record of those journal entries both to study and to remember my students by. We had agreed, though, that the journals were private and confidential, and I made no photocopies of what we had written in them. Moreover, the journals belonged to the students, and they kept them when they were full or when the term ended. If their children or grandchildren grow up to be linguists, maybe they can then conduct a more rigorous, empirical study of the efficacy of the use dialogue journals in learning to read and write in our ESL literacy class.

I do feel, however, that I learned certain things about using dialogue journals, which I would like to summarize here. First, dialogue with your students needs to begin before you start to use dialogue journals. It's not easy to strike up a correspondence with someone you know little or nothing about, even if you are literate and know how to write letters. Teachers need to know their students to be able to establish a meaningful connection with them in the dialogue journal—the writing should be an extension of a dialogue that has already begun in the teacher-student relationship. Second, the strategies used with neoliterate students for writing in dialogue journals should promote movement toward independent writing in the target language. You need to make sure that the tasks you give students in their dialogue journals correspond to their developmental level so they can have the satisfaction of successfully reading and writing something. At the same time, you need to try to reduce their dependence on you for what they write. With new writers, this may not be easy, since a student's developmental level and degree of dependence or independence are linked.

Finally, time is a critical element. Students need to have enough time in class to write in their journals without feeling pressured, if they are to get anything out of the experience. Finally, you can't rush a non-literate ESL student toward literacy, English proficiency, or independence. No matter how innovative your methods and techniques, it will take time— and patience, imagination, and perseverance.

Reference

Krashen, S. K. (1982). *Principles and practices in second language acquisition*. London: Pergamon Press.

11

Features of Semiliterate Writing: One Student's Development

Julietta Davis
Ravenswood City School
Palo Alto, California

At the Spanish Education Development (SED) Center in Washington, DC, where I was an ESL instructor in the Adult Education Program from 1985-1987, approximately 40% of the students in my program were semiliterate; that is, they knew that letters and words on paper had meaning, although they were not always able to decipher them. Half of the ESL students had had less than six years of formal schooling in their home countries. Their literacy level in Spanish was often low, resulting in reading and writing difficulties in English.

To develop these students' writing, we gave them controlled activities to develop their letter and word formation skills, which they hadn't always mastered, as well as opportunities to express themselves fluently in writing in more extended text. Moving along a continuum from controlled to free-writing activities, we worked on four types of writing: discrete-item activities, controlled compositions, paragraphs, and dialogue journals.

Students did discrete-item activities such as punctuation and spelling exercises and writing letters in print and cursive form to become aware of and practice basic writing features and to add them to their repertoire of writing skills. In controlled composition, which consists of following a model and altering parts of it, students worked on these same skills in a longer text. Paragraph writing was an opportunity for students to use what they had learned in semi-controlled writing to express ideas of their own. Finally, dialogue journals were the freest type of writing that students did, because neither the topic nor structure was controlled. Students might choose to write about any subject and in any form in the dialogue journal. It was our belief that using these four types of writing in the classroom would provide a bridge from learned items to free expression in writing.

Curious about changes that might occur over time in the free writing of these relatively beginning writers, I decided to study the dialogue journals of Maruja, a student from Peru who had been studying at the SED Center for over a year. Looking through early entries, I noticed four prominent features in the beginning stages of her dialogue journal writing, features that are easily quantifiable and are common among students with formal education deficits.

1. **"Pause points."** These are small dots that appear between words and in the middle of lines when students rest their pencils after laboriously writing a word. They are steps in the evolution of punctuation, often appearing where commas or other internal punctuation will be in later writing.

2. **Interchanged capital and small letters.** Capital and small letters are interspersed within sentences and even within individual words, one among a series of errors that take place in the writing of semiliterate students on the letter level.

3. **Mixture of printing and cursive writing.** Printing and cursive writing are used interchangeably within sentences or words, one among many types of errors that occur on the word level.

4. **Incorrect connection or division of words.** Separate words are connected, or individual words are divided into parts. These developmental errors occur along a continuum of changes that take place over time on the word level. For example, beginning nonliterate students often copy words in a single line without any spaces between words. Over time they begin to write words with some spaces in between, and finally, with a space between every word.

There are, of course, many more features of the writing that could be studied, including the content, expression of ideas, organization, and various types of complexity. This study is a first attempt at examining development, focusing on the form of writing. I studied these four features in Maruja's dialogue journal entries over ten months' time, comparing her first six consecutive entries, from July 1 to August 19, 1985, with her last six consecutive entries, from March 20 to April 10, 1986. I focused on her dialogue journals rather than her other writing because this was where she wrote regularly and spontaneously, without as much self- or teacher-monitoring or correction, providing an indication of development in the freest written context.

I found a remarkable reduction in pause points between the two sets of entries, with 21 pause points occurring in the 328 word early set and only 8 pause points in the 440 words in the later set. Even though Maruja wrote more in the later sample, she produced only around one-third as many pause points.

Use of capital and small letters also evolved from the first set of entries to the second. While the first set contained 95 examples of incorrectly placed capital or small letters in the sample of 328 words, the second set contained only half as many errors of this kind—50 in the 440-word sample. Maruja's writing had changed from a jumble of letter types with capital letters in any position in the word, to words made up mostly of small letters placed where they belonged. In the beginning, she always wrote "F" and "K," and usually wrote "T," as capitals. By the last entry, the correct use of capital and small forms of these letters had developed fully.

Similar changes took place in Maruja's printing and cursive writing. Oddly enough, she began by using predominantly cursive writing. Instead of connecting letters, however, she left spaces between them in a word and interspersed a few printed letters. Her last entry was primarily printed, with a few cursive letters sprinkled in. She had experimented with these two ways of writing and opted for printing. Changes back and forth from cursive to printing both on the word and sentence level were still evident in her last entry, but were much less frequent.

The last feature I examined was the connection of two words into one or the separation of a single word into two. Although this is a typical feature of many semiliterate students' initial writing, few examples occurred in Maruja's journal entries. She separated "same times" (sometimes) and combined "ofcurse" (of course) in the first set of entries and showed very little change in this feature over time, with only scattered examples in the second set.

The four features that I followed in this one student's writing seem to represent points along a continuum of developmental progress in writing. Pause points may be illustrative of punctuation development. The interchange of capital and small letters and the mixing of cursive and printed writing may represent a stage in the development of letter formation. The inappropriate connection and division of words may represent evolution on a word level.

Other features, representative of the development of writing on a sentence and discourse level, could also be identified and followed. The features I have chosen to look at offer educators an easy way to observe the evolution of student writing in dialogue journals.

It is unclear whether all the differences I found in Maruja's writing were due to the many opportunities she had to experiment with writing afforded by the journal, to her examination of her teacher's entries to her, to other class activities, or to a combination of factors. However, teachers considering using dialogue journals in an adult literacy program may find the results of this effort encouraging. At a minimum, dialogue journal writing appears to provide an opportunity to use writing features learned and practiced in more controlled exercises. It may also provide a place to acquire new features in an enjoyable, free-writing context.

Note

A similar version of this article was first printed in *Dialogue*, 3(3), September, 1986. It is reproduced with permission.

Hi, Melody
Answers to your questions
I think all the students have learned strategies from
one another. We've discussed some and could probably
do more in that department.

Tutors journals do seem to be a good means of communication. Also, it makes me think more about what
I'm doing. So yes, let's continue them.

Ideas
Enclosed is an article from the "Times" maybe you
saw it. That interests me because I see it in some
of my students. One, at least has a learning disability
and has had problems with the law. Would it be possible
to have someone (an expert) talk to us (tutors) and
give us some help?

Hello Linda,
    I read the article. Thanks for sharing it.
I love reading everything I can about this field.
I may be able to arrange for a speaker on this
in the new year but in the meantime I do have
some other articles on this subject to share with
you. There are some questions I have about this article
— or rather about the points it raises. I
wonder what they classify as a "learning disability" and they use the term "special
education" in seemingly conflicting ways. What
do you think?
    Melody

Part IV

Training Teachers and Tutors

A major concern in literacy education is to develop the professional status of the literacy teacher. Because literacy has for so long been addressed as a crisis that could be cured by the quick fix of a few missing basic skills that adults failed to acquire in grade school, there has been a common misconception that any literate person could become an effective teacher with little or no training. Especially with the influx of new immigrants who have received little or no prior schooling in any language, this attitude is changing. But, the struggle to provide appropriate and sufficient training for adult literacy educators (even if already trained as teachers of younger children) continues.

In this context, this section describes how dialogue journals can be used in training programs, to provide the same kind of empowerment for teachers that they do for students. What is essential for the development of competence in any area of human life is not the simple presentation of information, but the presence of another person, actively participating with the learner at critical times to model, guide, and reflect on performance. Dialogue journal writing can facilitate this guidance within teacher and tutor training programs.

Dialogue journals in the context of a training program can facilitate the development of mutual trust and the modeling of personal strengths and coping strategies needed in the target activity (in this case, becoming a competent literacy instructor or tutor). Dialogue journals provide mediated assistance to enable the learner to acquire these strategies. This relationship is captured by the metaphor of a "cognitive apprenticeship," the joint participation of a learner and a more competent person in a mutual task. The articles in this section by Schneider and Balliro are an excellent guide for literacy trainers in beginning this cognitive apprenticeship with their students.

12

Dialogue Journals in Teacher Education

Lenore Balliro
Adult Literacy Resource Institute
Roxbury Community College
Boston, Massachusetts

In recent years, dialogue journal writing has become increasingly popular as a way to promote students' literacy development. It has been used in ESL, bilingual and biliteracy classes, with children in whole language programs, with adults in community-based literacy programs, and in college-level ESL writing classes. Although the journal writing takes a variety of forms, and teachers are often in disagreement about the "rules" governing its use, there seems to be an underlying assumption that prompts its use and keeps it going: This type of writing allows for real communication. It acts as a heuristic for thinking and knowing. It allows for the struggle required to make meaning through language—particularly a new language. It lets students work at their own pace. It provides each of us—students and teachers—a vehicle for knowing each other not only in terms of language and writing proficiency, but also in terms of our needs, interests, fears, and strengths.

In addition to its use directly with students, dialogue journal writing also can be effective in teacher education and staff and program development. In this article, I discuss briefly three different ways that I have used dialogue journal writing for these purposes. One involves constructing an experience with dialogue journals to introduce teachers to the process so they will initiate it in their classrooms with their students. Another involves using dialogue journal writing to facilitate communication and cooperation among program coordinators and teachers in adult education programs. A third is the use of dialogue journal writing in a graduate ESL methodology class for prospective and practicing teachers.

Introducing Teachers to Dialogue Journal Writing

From my experience as an ESL Literacy Specialist at the Adult Literacy Resource Institute in Boston, I have found that for every teacher who has experimented with dialogue journal writing, there are several who have not heard of it and are mystified by the concept. This is particularly true for ESL teachers who often have had a more traditional, grammar-based orientation to instruction. To introduce the idea to adult education teachers and demonstrate its value, it is important to walk them through the use of this type of writing and then to explore the rationale for and details of implementation.

In a variety of workshops, I have introduced dialogue journal writing by having written dialogue serve a central communicative purpose—to introduce participants to each other. (This idea is an adaptation of one developed by Dennis Sayers of the Multifunctional Resource Center at Brown University.) When teachers enter the workshop, I give each one a "blue book," exam books used in university courses, with a slip of paper inside containing simple instructions. The instructions tell each person to pair up with someone she doesn't know. Each member of the pair writes for three minutes, introducing herself to the partner. After three minutes, I ask the participants to stop, exchange journals, read the partner's entry, then respond to it. The journals are exchanged two more times, so that dialogue is begun.

After this experience, each participant introduces her partner to the whole group, telling what she learned about her from their written exchange. Next we spend some time discussing the process itself. How was this experience like talking? How was it different? Most participants have said that they valued the uninterrupted time to say something in a more "protected" way than if they had had to introduce themselves orally. Others have commented that they paid attention to the content and not the surface features of their partners' entries. Others have said that they were excited to get a dialogue going, looked forward to getting a response back, and wished the activity had not ended so quickly.

The next step is engaging teachers in a discussion of the potential value of dialogue journal writing and how they might integrate the approach into their classroom instruction. At this stage, it is important to connect the qualities of the experience that the teachers valued (uninterrupted time to write, opportunity for one-on-one communication, dialogue that was meaningful) to what their students might also value from such an approach. Details for implementation ("mechanics") need to be discussed also, and handouts with a summary of essential information and a resource list for further reading (for example, Hill, 1988; Peyton, 1987; see also Dialogue Journal Resources at the end of this volume) can be provided. Finally, it is important to discuss how the workshop experience with dialogue journal writing can be adapted with the teachers' own students. Ideally, teachers can go back to their classrooms, try out the process for a few weeks, then reconvene in another workshop/teacher sharing format to exchange experiences, frustrations, and ideas for what works.

Maintaining Contact Between Teachers and Program Coordinators

A second use of dialogue journal writing with teachers is among teaching and program staff in an adult education agency or school setting. In this context, the journal can serve at least two valuable functions: The exchange of program information and details among staff, and reflection on experiences of teaching and learning. As director of a Workplace ESL/Literacy project in New Bedford and Fall River, Massachusetts, I was faced with the endemic problem of program fragmentation: Many of the teachers worked only part time, classes were held in various sites, teachers worked very different schedules, and so on. Our staff meetings were often consumed by "housekeeping" details because the funding and reporting requirements of the program were so complex. As the program director, I was also the curriculum developer, teacher trainer, and sometimes a teacher myself. Though I tried to visit and participate in teachers' classes, it was not always possible. Particularly in the first year of the program, when we were just starting up, there was little time for quality staff development.

The teachers and I agreed to keep dialogue journals as a way to keep in touch and to share insights into teaching and learning. At the same time, I wanted to make sure that teachers did not become overburdened by something they viewed as an additional requirement. I asked all of the teachers to start a notebook where they would keep their planning notes for class, and then record reflections on what had actually happened in class. They were encouraged to discuss things that worked as well as problems that came up—from lack of chalk in the classroom to problematic teaching/learning issues. I collected the journals and responded to them in writing, sometimes with specific references to additional resources, sometimes with suggestions for follow-up, sometimes with questions, and at other times just to share my own struggles as an educator.

One teacher expanded the content of her journal beyond class plans, to include snippets of conversations that came up in class and interesting issues that were introduced by the students and not officially part of the planned curriculum guide. We examined this writing as a staff and agreed that the issues discussed were more reflective of students' needs and interests than those included in our initial curriculum plans. We decided to adapt the curriculum to student needs that we could identify and record. For example, based on some observations and dialogue collected by one teacher, we developed realistic units to help students ask for a better piecework rate in their factory, something we could not find in any commercially prepared materials on the world of work. In this context, the journals served as logs and field notes as well as vehicles for communication.

Reflecting with Prospective Teachers on Their Learning

Finally, as part-time instructor of a graduate class in ESL methodology at Rhode Island College, I have asked the students to keep a dialogue journal with me as a way to reflect on their readings, classroom experiences, and practicum experience (tutoring a linguistic minority student in conversational English, literacy, biliteracy, or any combination that fit the situation). Sometimes students responded to specific questions I posed about the readings, but reflection on the practicum was open-ended. I wrote back to each of the students' entries. After a few weeks, most of us were looking forward to the exchange of notebooks. The process allowed for a one-to-one communication that would have been impossible otherwise, with limited face-to-face opportunities for inter-action. These dialogue journals yielded rich information in ways that continued to surprise and delight me as an instructor and conversation partner. I felt we were constructing knowledge together as we tackled both theoretical and pragmatic issues through our writing. Others have written about their use of dialogue journal writing in ESL methodology courses, with different approaches, which have also proven successful (cf. *Dialogue*, September, 1988).

Conclusion

Although I haven't tried it, I think that dialogue journal writing between teachers themselves could also prove useful as a way to promote teacher sharing. In my new position as coordinator of a regional staff development project in Massachusetts (System for Adult Basic Education Support, SABES), I hope to experiment with this idea. The value of the dialogue journal, whether between teacher and student, teacher and teacher, student and student, teacher and program director, or other combinations of writers or readers, experienced or inexperienced, is the same. It locates the production of written language within a context of genuine communication and the social construction of knowledge.

References

Hill, S. (1988). *Dialogue Journals*. New York: Literacy Assistance Center.

Interactive writing in teacher education. (1988, September). *Dialogue*, 5(2).

Peyton, J. K. (1987). *Dialogue journal writing with limited-English-proficient students*. Washington, DC: ERIC Clearinghouse on Languages and Linguistics.

13

Extending the Dialogue: Making Connections Between Learning and Teaching

Melody Schneider
Centers for Reading and Writing
New York Public Library
New York, New York

It is usually after a long day of tutorials at our adult literacy center that I appreciate the value of tutor-staff dialogue journals. With 60 students and 15 tutors, it is hard to know who needs what. I stuff the journals in my bag on my way out the door thinking I'll read them at home that night or the next morning, but I usually don't wait. Standing on the subway platform, I reach into my bag and pull them out. One of Linda's students made a breakthrough tonight, and Bruce is using some new spelling strategies. Another tutor is dealing with one student dominating the group. In the chaotic world of our center, the journals provide a sense of order. Sharing dialogue journals with my tutors has become one of my favorite parts of my job. Sharing dialogue journals has created a link between staff and tutors that did not exist before.

In this article, I show how tutor-staff dialogue journals are used at one of the Centers for Reading and Writing (CRW) of the New York Public Library. I discuss some of the benefits and drawbacks we have experienced and how the use of dialogue journals has enriched our learning community.

Getting Started

My first experience with dialogue journal writing was not as a staff member, but several years ago as a new volunteer tutor with Literacy Volunteers of New York City. As with most beginning tutors, I was nervous and not sure what I was doing. A few weeks after I began, my site coordinator, Marilyn Collins, asked me to keep a journal with her. In it, I could write about my lessons, ask questions, whatever I wished. I was to leave the journal in a designated box, and she would read my entry and write back. This idea made me very nervous, and I had a lot of hesitations about writing: I did not have time; I did not want to write; Was I going to be evaluated?; What if I was not doing this right? But, Marilyn explained that this was a way for her to support me and everyone else, so I agreed. I stayed a few minutes after my tutoring session, thought about how it had gone, and wrote.

When I picked up my journal before the next session, I saw that in her response, Marilyn had reflected back some of my thoughts and added some encouragement. Soon I looked forward to those letters. I came to rely on the support they gave me, the suggestions Marilyn offered, and the questions she asked that made me look at instruction in new ways.

Several years later, when I came on staff at the CRW, I saw how difficult it was to give support to so many tutors and students. I wanted to alleviate the isolation of the tutorial groups and create more of a community at the Center. I remembered my dialogue journal with Marilyn and decided to try them with our tutors. Handing out blank wire-bound notebooks, I explained, much as Marilyn had, what we would be doing. Some tutors looked nervous, some skeptical, and some very interested. We agreed to try them for a month.

That first night I wasn't sure what to expect. Initial entries were brief. Tutors asked questions or reported on their session, and I tried to encourage and provide new ideas or offer suggestions, as Marilyn had first done with me.

October 27, 1988

The group chose Tales of Mystery and the Unknown as the next book to read together. The first story was difficult for them, but a great story. It's funny (not really) Bob has trouble reading, but his comprehension is excellent, while Carl can string the words together, but rarely knows what they mean. I guess it's a good balance because they do help one another out.

At home Bob is rereading the book we just finished--he feels he missed some parts. Carl is reading a book about Viet Nam that he got from here. Richard has been out this week. He took a second job and has to work out his schedule.

November 1, 1988

Hi Linda

I'm curious. Have Bob and Carl ever discussed what they do when they read and compare their "styles"—maybe get some ideas about what strategies each other use? They seem like an ideal pair. Very lucky....

We were all rather hesitant and careful at this point, but we had gotten a start.

Can We Keep This Up?

As the month went on, the entries became more involved. I was learning new things about tutors and their groups, and I soon saw the effect my responses had in creating an ongoing dialogue. I was really enjoying the journals and didn't want them to end. Fortunately, the tutors were enjoying them, too, so we decided to continue. Through the continued sharing of ideas, articles, and strategies, our relationships at the Center began to change. Tutors and staff became collaborators. The following exchange comes from our second month of writing.

December 1, 1988

Hi, Melody

Answers to your questions

I think all the students have learned strategies from one another. We've discussed some and could probably do more in that department.

Tutor journals do seem to be a good means of communication. Also, it makes me think more about what I'm doing. So yes, let's continue them.

Ideas

Enclosed is an article from the "Times" maybe you saw it. That interests me because I see it in some of my students. One, at least has a learning disability and has had problems with the law. Would it be possible to have someone (an expert) talk to us (tutors) and give us some help?

Hello Linda

I read the article. Thanks for sharing it. I love reading everything I can about this field. I may be able to arrange for a speaker on this in the New Year but in the meantime I do have some other articles on this subject to share with you. There are some questions I have about this article--or rather about the points it raises. I wonder what they classify as a "learning disability" and they use the term "special education" in seemingly conflicting ways. What do you think?

Melody

Over time, as we became more comfortable in our new roles as collaborators, the uses for the journals continued to grow. We shared problems and frustrations, complained, asked advice, and shared breakthroughs:

May 13, 1989

Melody,

I need your advice about Carl. He has now used up his 3 absences--even though two of the nights were not rainy. I don't feel that he should be excused from any more absences, but with a month and a half to go, the chances are good that they'll occur. Shall I ask him or warn him that he'll have to leave the group? Shall I open the problem to the group? What do you think?

Linda

Hi Linda

What did you and Carl decide? It's really tough to be hard line about these contracts but it's also important to stress the commitment. The group's input could certainly help.

June 8, 1989

Melody

Sorry I haven't been "communicating" via the journal lately, but it's been crazy and these ankles leave me a bit ragged around the edges sometimes. I did want to tell you about a breakthrough I think Carl is making; he is beginning to read with expression! I mean, he is actually stopping at periods and seeing that words belong in phrases. I complimented him on it last time and could see him really trying after that. More later-

Hi Linda

What good news. I think it's important to make the connection between our reading understanding and our writing. What are the differences in what he does when he reads silently and orally?

94

Some tutors were reluctant to write, fearing they would be evaluated. In fact, in the beginning I did think about the journals as a way to know how our tutors were doing. Were they doing it "right?" Who needed observation?, and so on. I slowly learned though, that if the journals were to serve as a place for tutors to explore their learning and teaching processes, my responses needed to be free of evaluation. I learned to keep my responses as reflective as possible while still providing suggestions, and I found I needed to change the tone of my questions from "Why are you doing it that way?" to "How do you find this strategy works?"

Why Don't You Write?

Once a journal with a tutor is begun, the biggest problem with maintaining the exchange is time. Some tutors write after their session or come in early. Some take the journal home or write during their session. But, for others these options aren't possible, so they write infrequently or not at all. Like students, they usually arrive at their tutorial session just after work and then want to get home immediately afterward. Their lives are very busy, and it's hard to find time outside the tutorial to write. Several tutors have expressed this frustration. As one said, "When I've written I really liked it, but I just can't fit it in." We try to keep up verbal communication in those cases, by my visiting the tutorial groups more or talking with the tutors informally before or after the session. Having the journals with most of the tutors makes it easier to support those who do not write in this way.

Time is not the only drawback. In many cases, tutors prefer face-to-face communication. They get an immediate response, can elaborate on their questions or ideas, and feel that the contact is more personal.

There has also been some concern among tutors about confidentiality: worry about who might pick the journal up and read it. I try to arrange the exchange so the tutors are comfortable. They can hand the journal to me personally or leave it in our Journal Box.

"I Really Enjoyed Tonight."

Since the journals were working so well in the tutorial sessions, I realized they would fit perfectly into our new tutor trainings. They would give tutors their first taste of writing—something we encourage them to do along with their students—and begin the communication process with me and other staff. I also wanted my new colleague on staff, Tom Peele, to become involved in the dialogues as a way to familiarize him with everyone and integrate him into our community.

At the initial session of a recent new tutor training, we passed out the journals and asked for entries every session. We wondered if these entries would differ from those of our current tutors and if doing them from the start would help new tutors feel more confident in their work and perhaps ease the transition from the safety of the training to their tutorials. These entries, written the first night, indicated that the journals gave us a good start.

> *October 3, 1989*
>
> *I've never taught before, so I am concerned about how I will be conveying the knowledge and skills that go into reading and writing. I feel very reassured about the practicum and the program by this beginning. It is very open. I particularly like the idea behind these journals, they are an excellent way to exercise writing as an informal means of communication. I like the shared quality of the dialogue journals. What you say to someone and what you write to them are different in many complex ways and to explore this while teaching others to read and write will certainly open up my thinking about it.*
>
> *Matthew*

October 31, 1989

I really enjoyed tonight. When I was coming here I was nervous because I thought a lot more was expected of me than actually was. This is a process and tonight made me feel a real part of that process. When I read that handout about the journals I realized how much we miss ourselves and each other by the roles we assign ourselves. I think this is about taking the blinders off and re- evaluating how we perceive those roles.

Patricia

While the journals provided a place for all of our tutors to share their observations and reflect in depth on the learning process, the new tutors used them primarily to express doubts and clarify parts of the training:

October 6, 1989

What a pleasure to write in my journal again. I have been working on my piece for class on my computer at work using a lot of different methods that we talked about in class: cut and paste, doodle, etc. So I was playing and not having any fun because of that critical voice inside my head. I read these handouts and the literature and am really taken with how much I identify. I think I am beginning to remember a little of the learning process that I went through. I blocked most of it out because of fear and feelings of inadequacy. Anyway, I did not understand phonics when it was taught to me and I thought that there was something wrong with me or that this carried over to my belief in myself as a writer and a reader. The part of this that I am wondering about is how to work with an individual and not disturb other members of the group. I asked about taking students aside and having them read to you etc. Is there space besides the round tables to work from? Do you have to do everything as a group mini lesson? I am can see how the negotiation process is so important.

Patricia

Journals and Our Community

Through the journals, we have built a cohesive community of new and experienced tutors and staff, in which we provide support for each other, make instructional suggestions, share frustrations, and suggest books or other materials some of us may not know about. We all look forward to reading them, and often we ask each other, "Did you write?," and are disappointed when we haven't. By knowing what different groups are doing, I can bring groups with similar interests together, refer tutors to others with similar problems, and brainstorm for solutions. The journals encourage tutors to reflect on their learning in the same way that students do, therefore providing a shared experience. I also ask tutors to share successful strategies with each other, and so we expand our field of "experts."

Linda's journal comment reflects the feeling that many of us have about the value of the journals in our adult literacy program.

January 16, 1990

Offhand I can't think of anything that doesn't appeal to me about this journal. Sometimes, I don't have much time for it, but that's not because I don't want to write in it. On the positive side, I like it because it gives me an ongoing way of communicating with you and focusing on my work here. This place fairly jumps with ideas and enthusiasm and it's good to feel a part of it and to work out various approaches, ideas, strategies etc. The Journal is one outlet for all that.

Dear Kathleen, Thank you! My husband worry about me. Because I came to S.F. I always was a little homesick. He often tells me he will takes me go back visit my father, mother and sisters next years. I hope so.

I often write letters to my mother. I telled her about my family in S.F. And about school. I have new friends here. But I miss them in China. Sometimes I was homesick and I cry a little. I very miss my mother.

Dear Jing, I remember the first time I was far away from my mother and father. I was very homesick and I cried a lot. I'm happy that I had such nice parents. They "were" my mother and father. They changed into my friends. Next time you write to your mother, tell her hello for me.

Dear Kathleen, Thank you! My mother must thank you for you. I think you are a good teacher, a good wife and a good mother. Over the weekend you worked in the garden, and cooked, etc. On the weekend I visited my sister in law.

Part V

Benefits for Students and Teachers

Teachers using an open-ended educational approach cite a wide variety of benefits derived from the use of such an approach in their particular context. In this section, Paul Jones reviews some of the benefits of dialogue journal writing, focusing on adult students and their teachers. His review is based on his own experience, and on a survey of teachers in the field.

The benefit of dialogue journals most often cited is the opportunity for teachers and students to get to know each other in new ways, to develop greater rapport and mutual understanding, to expand and deepen the communication they have, in other forms, elsewhere. Development in language proficiency and in writing and reading ability, although often very visible and initially the impetus for doing the writing, for many become secondary to the sense of improved overall communication.

In addition to this benefit, which has become almost universally acknowledged, engagement in interactive writing of any kind seems to make evident and reinforce some valuable but often overlooked basic truths about teaching and learning.

The first of these truths is that students' language and cultural backgrounds are an essential part of their learning. Students' own language and culture are not only the foundation on which to build new knowledge and abilities, but also a rich resource for any educational program. As Jones points out here, in writing that draws from students' lives, "human culture in all its diversity can reveal itself."

Second, writing is exploratory and provocative. It is never finished, but serves as a next step upon which further steps can be taken. It is provoked by previous speech or writing and in turn provokes more. Much school-based writing conceals the dynamic nature of the writing process, and students can be deceived into thinking that writing must always be perfect and final. Dialogue journal writing gives students, and teachers, opportunities to explore writing framed in an open-ended dialogue.

Third, teachers, as well as students, are writers and learners. We are all continually learning, and we all need to be reading and writing. Dialogue journals get us, the teachers, writing and, we hope, learning.

14

The Various Benefits of Dialogue Journals

Paul Jones
Putney, Vermont

Dialogue journal writing can benefit both students and teachers in many ways. In this chapter, I discuss some of those benefits, turning first to the realm of student-teacher relationships, then separately to the specific benefits for students and for teachers. My observations come from my own experiences teaching adults learning English as a second language, from extensive research on dialogue journal use, and from my interviews with many adult ESL teachers.

Dialogue journals, if used with commitment and openness, provide both participants with tremendous opportunities for growth and learning. The writing enables students and teachers to get to know each other in entirely new ways, which often leads to greater rapport and mutual understanding. The potential to foster stronger relationships is perhaps the most compelling and captivating feature of dialogue writing.

For students, in particular, the writing can lead to significant changes in attitudes that may affect their learning. It can also promote improvement of second language reading and writing skills, and may help students acquire the written forms and syntax of a new language. In many cases, students can also use the journals as a forum in which to discuss and solve problems.

Teachers stand to gain from the interaction as well. The journals can be a powerful tool both for individualizing instruction and for planning lessons. Dialogue writing can also teach teachers a great deal about other cultures, and may help them to improve their own writing. Finally, dialogue journals can be inspirational to teachers, bringing or renewing meaning and joy to their work in the classroom.

Let's begin by looking at the heart of adult ESL classrooms—student-teacher relationships—and at how those relationships may be affected by dialogue writing.

New Communication, Rapport, and Understanding Between Teacher and Students

Dialogue journals enable teacher and student to get to know each other in ways that simply are not possible otherwise. They do this, in the words of Joy Peyton and Leslee Reed, by opening "an entirely new channel of communication" (Peyton & Reed, 1990).

In class there is rarely sufficient time to talk to each student regularly or in much depth. Moreover, students may be embarrassed or afraid to speak openly with a teacher in front of others. Carmen, an advanced ESL student from Mexico, explained during an interview how dialogue journal writing allowed her to communicate with her teacher in ways that were not possible before:

> *I like writing back and forth to the teacher a lot. Since I'm not very sure of myself to talk, I get nervous and don't talk much in class. On paper I find it easier to express myself. I know her, I can ask her questions, I like it. I feel that the student and the teacher get closer that way.*

The practice also enables less reticent, even aggressive students to exchange ideas at length with the teacher, without monopolizing limited class time.

ESL students in this country often have limited contact with Americans. This is particularly true for immigrants and refugees, whose boss or landlord may be the only native English speaker with whom they deal regularly. Through dialogue journals, their ESL teacher may become the first American with whom they can communicate openly and positively in an ongoing fashion. Looking back on the semester, Carmen added:

> ... there were times when I don't have anyone here to talk to, so I could say many things—like a purging of things inside...

Such openness can benefit teachers as much as students. As Kathy, a young ESL instructor, explained:

> I learned a lot about the psychological states of students who were struggling with or adapting to North American culture and I used these insights in my teaching. I became more sensitive to what was taking place inside the students.

As most of us know from our own lives, open communication with others can lead to stronger, closer relationships. To be sure, dialogue journals don't always lead to close friendships. They rarely fail, however, to expand and deepen communication between teacher and student, and, at the very least, usually enable both parties to view each other with new understanding and respect.

Lasting attachments of one sort or another between teachers and students who write in dialogue journals are not uncommon. As another teacher told me, "I still correspond with students and feel that attachment (and subsequent writing) is a *direct* outgrowth of our 'written dialogues' during their time here."

Leslee Reed, who has used dialogue journals with children for roughly twenty years, has summed up the interpersonal benefits that are possible in this way:

> I would like for everyone to see the love that goes into the journals, not just on my part, but on the children's part, too. The love, the respect, the mutuality of goals, the feelings that we develop for each other....Every year, the last week of school, I think I will never do

journals again because I end up being rather tearful, and I don't want to say goodbye....And yet,...this, too, is a growing experience. I think any teacher who allows herself to get this involved with individuals can't help but be enriched by just learning about each child.

The feeling that I care for you and you care for me has to be there; it has to be there in school. The people who say that a good teacher doesn't get emotionally involved with students are missing something very important. The first step is to be warm, personal and friendly—you have to be emotionally involved with those with whom you work and those whom you teach. You have to love them, each one of them.

(Reed, 1988, pp. 71-72)

Some Benefits for Students

Conversation is the laboratory and workshop of the student.
Ralph Waldo Emerson

Obviously, no two individuals will be affected by dialogue journal writing in precisely the same way, and some may not be perceptibly affected at all. In general, however, I see at least four possible ways that adult ESL literacy students can benefit from dialogue journal writing. First, dialogue journals can promote changes in student attitudes toward the second language, toward school, and toward self. Second, the practice can help students improve their reading and writing abilities in the new language. Third, dialogue journal writing may promote the acquisition of the forms and syntax of the written language. Finally, exchanging information and opinions with the teacher may help students solve problems both in and out of school.

Changes in Attitudes

Perhaps the most striking benefit of dialogue writing is its ability to help adults overcome their fear of the written form of a second language and increase their self-confidence and willingness to write. This is no mean feat. For many of us, learning to write is a challenge frought with frustration and fear, even in our native language. Yet, what Jerome Bruner has called "the daunting vastness of a blank page and the inherent terror that it evokes for the novice writer" (Bruner, 1988, p. viii) can appear that much worse when it involves a new language.

Dialogue journals offer students a path through their fear by allowing them to write about things meaningful to them in a nonevaluated, nonthreatening context (Shuy, 1980). Many students who initially feel hesitant or afraid to write in a second language find, often to their surprise, that they actually enjoy writing back and forth with their teacher. Pretty soon, perhaps without realizing it, they've developed the confidence that comes from having done something new and having done it well.

The effect can be dramatic. María, an advanced ESL student whose native language was Spanish, put it clearly:

> *When I look at my journal I feel good just to see that I have a lot of pages written in English. That makes me feel—Oh, Wow! I feel good. It seems—I can't believe that—they are mine. I feel more confident about writing in English now than I did before. The biggest thing is that I lost my fear of writing in English.*

Written dialogue may open the door to greater willingness to participate in all aspects of a class. Zhi Tian, a Chinese student of mine in her late twenties (student permission was granted to use the entries shown here, and pseudonyms are used), was often late to class and resisted participating in group activities. She seemed taciturn and even rude with her fellow students. Her first journal entry contained an apology.

*Dear Paul, Yesterday. I'm tired. I'm not to school. I'm
sorry. I live to school English.*

As the dialogue progressed, Zhi Tian told me about her family, her
work, and her feelings about being in America. She also took frequent
advantage of the opportunity to ask me questions, probably the first time
she had ever done so with a teacher. Here are a few examples:

*Where are you from? Is your family here in San Francisco?
Are you life to school?*

*How many sisters do you have? Do you like fortune
cookies?*

*I like American food! I like to cook. Do you like CHinese?
Do you like to be Chinese friend?*

As the dialogue unfolded, her behavior in class changed. She began
to come on time and participate more willingly. While I can't prove that
the dialogue journal writing caused these changes, it seemed to play a
major role.

Some researchers believe that the interaction may help increase
students' motivation not only to write, but more generally to study a
second language and go to school. In a study of deaf students' enrollment
in college preparatory English language classes at Gallaudet University,
Jana Staton (1985) found that students whose instructors used dialogue
journals were twice as likely to re-enroll for subsequent English classes
as students who didn't keep the journals. Kathleen Wolf noticed
something similar at Alemany College in San Francisco, where students
are routinely promoted into more advanced classes as less proficient
students arrive. During her first experience with dialogue journals there,
Wolf found that five students whom she wanted to promote adamantly
refused to leave her class. When asked why, they said they did not want
to stop writing with her in their notebooks. While factors other than
journal writing, such as teacher personality, may well have played a role
in both situations, it is clear that the writing was perceived very positively
by the students.

Improved Reading and Writing Skills

Most adult ESL programs in this country today, particularly those serving immigrants and refugees, focus heavily on oral skills. All too few students get the instruction and practice they need to improve their mastery of the written language. Part of the problem is that few instructors feel prepared to teach reading or writing. Many don't know where to start.

Dialogue journals can help address this problem in several ways. First, dialogue writing gives students extensive practice reading comprehensible texts in the new language. Second, it can help students build fluency in writing. Third, dialogue writing can help students begin to develop skills useful in more formal academic writing (Kreeft, 1984; Peyton, Staton, Richardson, & Wolfram, 1990; Vanett & Jurich, 1990). Moreover, the journals are relatively easy to use and to integrate into existing teaching approaches.

Improved second language reading skills.

It's wonderful to watch my students whenever I hand out their dialogue journals during class. Desks are pulled apart, heads go down, and the room grows palpably silent as they devour my latest entries.

Doing dialogue journals immerses students in frequent reading in the second language. Unlike many assigned texts, teacher entries are personalized and usually comprehensible. If something isn't clear, students either ask for clarification or respond in such a way that reveals the misunderstanding, allowing the teacher to clarify. Many adult students are, to say the least, apprehensive about reading in a second language. Within weeks of beginning dialogue journals, that fear can seem to melt away. Best of all, the confidence and facility that develop can stay with students, preparing them to go on successfully to a wide variety of other texts.

Jana Staton has explored a bit further the question of how dialogue journals compare to published reading texts as a way to build reading skills. In an interesting pilot study, she compared a teacher's dialogue journal entries with one student to a basal reader used by that student in the same class (Staton, 1986). She found that the journal entries were both linguistically more complex and cognitively more demanding than the basal reader, with more complex relationships between ideas, requiring greater inferencing and synthesis of information. Because this analysis was based on only one journal, more studies are needed. It seems clear, however, that dialogue journals afford most teachers a relatively simple way of breaking the reading barrier and of building skills that can help prepare students to go on to other texts.

Improved fluency in writing.

I once heard a high school ESL teacher make the following remark: "Dialogue journals? Oh, yeah, I've heard of that. I call it writing for fluency." The notion that dialogue writing builds fluency in writing has become almost a truism among teachers more or less familiar with the genre. However, "fluency" is a bit like "critical thinking"—an oft-wielded, not so often understood term that seems somehow to elude precise definition.

In lay terms, fluency is usually thought of as the ability to communicate fairly effectively and with ease. Shelly Gutstein, building on Charles Fillmore's (1979) criteria for fluency in speech, has proposed a more rigorous definition. She suggests that second language learners should satisfy the following four criteria to be considered "fluent" writers:

1. Write easily and quickly with few pauses;
2. Get meaning across in coherent, reasoned sentences (errors in form may occur as long as they don't interfere substantially with meaning);
3. Be able to use writing to express a wide range of language functions;
4. Be creative and imaginative in writing (e.g., use humor or metaphor) (Gutstein, 1987).

My own teaching and research, as well as the findings of other researchers (Kreeft, Shuy, Staton, Reed, & Morroy, 1984), show dialogue journal writing to be a likely way to help students improve in all four areas.

It seems to be the dialogue itself that makes this possible. As students read and respond to their teacher's comments in a nonthreatening, enjoyable context, they are pulled slowly but surely into ever deeper use of the written language. Almost without realizing it, students can begin to make progress in each of these four areas. Let's look in more detail at how this might happen.

María speaks for many adult students when she says that dialogue writing has helped her with the first skill—writing more easily:

> *In the beginning I was more worried about my grammar.*
> *Now not any more, now I'm worried about the theme. It's*
> *easier for me to write in English now than before. Maybe at*
> *the beginning I had to think a lot about what I wanted to talk*
> *about, but now I just start writing. I don't think about it.*
> *I think of the ideas, whatever came to my brain.*

I have found that many students begin by writing two or three sentences per entry. By mid-semester, they are writing a half or full page within the same amount of time. This observation, confirmed by numerous researchers (Peyton, Staton, Richardson, & Wolfram, 1990; Kreeft, 1984; Shuy, 1980), is another indication that the process of dialogue journal writing helps students to write more easily and quickly.

Second, conversing on paper certainly encourages students to get meaning across coherently. Misunderstandings on the part of either participant usually become evident during the course of the exchange and can be resolved in subsequent discussion. Such negotiation of meaning is intrinsic to the nature of human dialogue, particularly if that dialogue is extended over a long period of time.

Third, written dialogue lends itself naturally to the use of a wide variety of language functions, from reporting personal facts and opinions to asking questions, complaining, giving excuses, and expressing other communicative needs and desires (Shuy, 1988). Again, this happens in the normal course of conversation, as both people get to know each other and increasingly share information and ideas meaningful to them.

Finally, dialogue journals can be "a place to enjoy writing and play with language," in the words of one teacher. Students can be droll, witty, somber, cute, and even poetic in their writing. Metaphor often appears in their dialogue; a Polish student of mine who described her life as a "highway with exits but no on-ramps" is but one example. Learning to use language creatively is probably the most difficult of the four skills to acquire, however. Whether or not a student actually succeeds probably depends a lot on the personalities and styles of both student and teacher.

Just as someone learns to stay upright on a bicycle (and to ride more easily and quickly) by practicing, a language student doing dialogue journals becomes more fluent in writing by actively communicating on paper. When it comes to improving fluency, dialogue writing can be learning by doing, in the best sense of the phrase.

A bridge to academic writing.

Recent research by Joy Kreeft Peyton and others suggests that dialogue journal writing involves numerous skills also required of more formal academic writing. In one case study, Kreeft (1984) showed how dialogue journal writing helped a young student learn to elaborate on topics, to write with awareness of his audience's interests and knowledge, and to write about topics new to his audience—all skills important in more formal essay writing. In a separate study comparing students' dialogue writing to their assigned compositions, Peyton et al. (1990) found that the journal writing was as linguistically complex, had as much extended topic elaboration, and was as high in text cohesion as the more formal writing. In some cases, the journal writing was more complex, elaborated, and cohesive than other writing by the same student.

Dialogue journal writing should not replace practice in writing formal prose. However, the journals can provide extensive practice in skills needed for other kinds of writing, in a context that is more enjoyable, less threatening, and more personally meaningful than is often true of assigned compositions. As such, they can serve as a bridge to other kinds of writing.

Acquisition of the Forms and Syntax of the Written Language

Language is like muscle. It grows with use. Dialogue writing immerses students in the use of written language, giving them both reason and means for growth in that language.

Interactive writing can promote the learning of written forms of language and syntax in at least two ways. First, the desire to communicate, to maintain the dialogue, gives students reason to consult, and study, correct forms of the new language. Second, the very act of communicating in writing may promote the unconscious acquisition of written linguistic structures, according to researchers (Burling, 1982;

111

Krashen, 1982; Kreeft et al., 1984). Let's now examine each possibility more closely.

Engaged in real dialogue, students are bursting with thoughts and ideas they want to get out, even though they may not have mastered the means to do so. The desire to express themselves may lead them to look up or ask the spelling or meaning of a word, or the correct use of a grammatical structure. I've often seen word translations in Chinese and Spanish scribbled in the margins of my responses; some of these words appear again and again in English in the students' subsequent writing.

I remember vividly José, an affable Salvadoran student who often seemed more interested in the other students than in the classwork. One day he approached me, almost apologetically, while the class was busy writing in their journals. "Excuse me," he asked in Spanish. "How do I say 'I am' for yesterday?" We hadn't yet covered past tense verb forms in class. I wrote what he wanted on the board. We discussed the concept of past tense and compared it to Spanish. He thanked me and returned to his seat. That evening, "wasn't" appeared in his latest entry.

José certainly did not master the use of the past tense of "to be" during that brief exchange. This wasn't even his first introduction to the concept of past tense. I felt, nonetheless, that this was a significant step in his learning. He had thoughts he wanted to express, and he knew that he didn't know how to do so clearly, so he asked.

Now let's consider the second possibility, namely that the written structures of a second language might be acquired subconsciously in the course of writing dialogue. This concept has been proposed by Jana Staton (in press), who argues for a process of written second language acquisition analogous to that envisioned by Krashen (1982) for oral language. In this view, a second language learner can assimilate written structures by actively communicating in writing with native speakers, providing that several criteria are met: The communication must be meaningful and interesting; "real" language must be used—e.g., the native speaker's language shouldn't be grammatically sequenced according to a pre-established plan; the written "input" received by the learner must be comprehensible but slightly more advanced structurally than his or her own writing; the interaction must be nonthreatening and comfortable for the student; and there must be opportunities for clarification and elaboration.

Staton suggests that dialogue journals meet these criteria. She shows how one teacher varies systematically the syntactic complexity and interactional features (e.g., consistent use of topic sentences to introduce new topics) of her writing according to her students' English proficiency, and compares these systematic variations to those identified by Long (1983) in native speaker/nonnative speaker (NS-NNS) speech. Staton concludes that a teacher's dialogue writing, like the "optimal input" of native-speaker (NS) speech, may promote the acquisition of the structures of written English.

Although the hypothesis is appealing, many mysteries remain. We still know relatively little about *how* "optimal input" might lead language to lodge in the subconscious, to become sufficiently owned by the brain so that it can be produced automatically, without conscious effort. Hopefully, as linguists and educators learn more about the ways in which adults acquire a second language, we will eventually understand more fully how dialogue journal writing might contribute to the subconscious, or automatic, acquisition of written language structures.

Discussing and Solving Problems

Written dialogues tend to evolve in stages. As students become more comfortable "conversing" with the teacher, their entries evolve from relatively dry descriptions of where they live, what they like, or what they have done to more involved discussions of important events, feelings, and problems. I have found that this transition usually takes four to eight weeks, writing with adult students from one to three times a week.

Some of the problems that students discuss in their journals are discrete and resolvable; others are more complex, ongoing, and not easily resolved. Depending on the teacher's willingness and ability to respond, students can benefit in a number of ways from these discussions. They may get the comfort and satisfaction that comes from sharing problems with another person, knowing that the person is really listening. Sometimes, the teacher may be able to offer a new perspective, ask questions, or give information that actually helps the students solve the problem.

Alicia, a widow in her thirties, discussed many aspects of her life with her teacher, Kathleen. Sometimes these involved relatively discrete problems, as in the following exchange:

113

March 15

*Dear Kathleen, this Weekend I don't Feel very good. because
I have a coold. What about you,?*

March 15

*Dear Alicia, Did you stay in bed over the weekend? Did you
have a fever?*

March 17

*Kathleen, I'm did a Little bit Feber I have bronchitis, but no
is problem for my, Bicause not have a Job here.*

March 20

*Alicia, I'm so sorry you're not feeling well. Many people
have bronchitis now.*

Other problems brought up by Alicia were more difficult. Whatever
the trouble, though, Kathleen listened and responded as an empathetic
friend.

Sometimes students discuss problems involving school. A student
who is always very late to a morning class may explain that he is
exhausted because he works a double night shift. Another student may
wonder "aloud" whether or not to change to a more advanced class. The
teacher can discuss these problems honestly with the student, perhaps
offering alternatives for consideration, or simply letting the student
know that she understands and accepts the situation.

Most recent immigrants and refugees enrolled in ESL programs in
this country are poor. Many face serious problems involving housing,
immigration, employment, family and emotional difficulties, neigh-
borhood violence, or health. Adult students often reveal these problems
in their journals. Some of these problems can and should be actively
addressed, yet the student may feel unable to handle them alone. This
can raise difficult issues for the teacher, who may feel that merely

"listening," while knowing of a serious, remediable situation, is uncomfortable at best, and at worst, unethical.

On the other hand, teachers must be cautious about personal involvement with their students' problems. Within refugee ESL circles, I have known teachers to complain that their efforts to help students became burdensome, involving them after hours in such activities as doing income taxes, calling (and sometimes "fighting" with) landlords, going to hospital emergency rooms, and even getting involved in family disputes. Such involvement can become exhausting, provoking cries of "burn out"; occasionally, as in some disputes, the involvement may actually become threatening to the teacher. In either case, the desire to help can at times lead teachers over the fine line between healthy concern and inappropriate involvement.

Frequently, the dilemma posed by wanting to do neither too little nor too much can be resolved by offering to be a referral source. The teacher can mention that he or she knows of a person or organization that might be able to help with a particular problem, giving the student the option of asking for the information.

Miguel, an adult student of mine, had been complaining for weeks that he wanted to quit his job, when he wrote this entry:

> *Yes. I want stay here in this country. But I have to know Inglish first, and about friends I have many friends and then that I have other problem. I don't have paper grin car. I don't have nathink. And the imigrashion maybe no more job for me.*

I suspected that Miguel could get himself in much deeper trouble by quitting his job, and felt that he might benefit from legal advice, so in my response I offered to refer him to an organization specializing in immigration work:

> *You are doing a good job learning English. If you study hard you will learn a lot of English quickly.....Maybe you should talk to an immigration lawyer. Do you know about the ____ (agency specializing in immigration assistance)? If you are interested, please talk to me after class.*

115

Miguel did not, in fact, know his rights under the new amnesty law. After class he asked for the name of the agency in question. They told him that he wasn't eligible for amnesty, but that a "grandfather" clause would effectively protect him as long as he stayed in the same job. He followed their advice, kept his job, and remained in the country.

A year earlier, also through our dialogue journal, I had referred another student who was in the country illegally to a similar agency. This woman, it turned out, was eligible for amnesty. After years of living in fear, unable to get out of a dead-end job or visit her family overseas, she at last became a legal resident and began to make important changes in her life.

The referral role requires that a teacher be informed about appropriate sources of assistance for specific issues, or at least know where to find that information. It expands the teacher's role somewhat to that of community liaison, yet protects him or her from either inappropriate involvement or unethical detachment. In the process, it enables the student to use the dialogue journal to help address specific problems.

Several students have told me that writing in their journals is "like a therapy." One French student explained:

> I learned a lot about...myself. Things came out of my sub-conscious in the writing almost like a therapy session (not necessarily personal revelations).

In many respects, dialogue journals function in something akin to the "understanding/listening" role of teachers in Community Language Learning (CLL), based on the work of Charles Curran (1976). That approach trains teachers in a special kind of listening, designed to put students at ease to discuss whatever is on their minds. In both CLL and dialogue writing, students are supported by knowing that their teacher is listening sincerely and sympathetically. Nonetheless, in dialogue writing it is crucial that neither the teacher nor the student perceive the teacher's role as that of therapist. Once that line is crossed, the teacher may be expected to meet needs that are both unrealistic and inappropriate.

Some teachers find that dealing with students' painful personal matters is the most difficult aspect of journal writing. Clearly, teachers must decide for themselves how involved to get. Teachers should not feel compelled to discuss students' personal lives if they don't want to. As in oral conversation, if a topic feels uncomfortably personal, the teacher should be able to find gentle, effective ways to steer the discussion in other directions.

Joy Peyton and Leslee Reed (1990) point out that students may occasionally reveal information indicating such serious or immediate danger to themselves or someone else that the teacher feels compelled to seek outside help, with or without consulting the student. Such action would obviously violate the confidentiality of the dialogue, and should therefore only be undertaken when it is clear that danger or harm may result to the student or to someone else if action is not taken.

Some Benefits for Teachers

Teachers stand to gain in many ways from using dialogue journals. As I'll show in the following pages, the writing can be a powerful tool for individualizing instruction, planning lessons, and solving problems in the classroom. But perhaps most important, dialogue writing teaches the teacher—about students as people, about their cultures, and thus about the world (Staton, Peyton, & Gutstein, 1986). It can even teach teachers about themselves. For some teachers, the writing has remarkable power to strengthen a sense of purpose in teaching, and to give or restore love and meaning to the work.

Individualizing Instruction
Every student is unique. No matter how much care is taken to place language students of similar proficiency together, the differences among individuals in the same class can be enormous. Being aware of and responding to those differences are two of the greatest challenges of classroom language teaching. Dialogue journals offer teachers a powerful means of meeting those challenges.

During class, especially in those with more than twenty-five students, most teachers are hard pressed to monitor closely each student's

117

abilities or progress. Dialogue journals can change that radically. They open a window on each student, allowing the teacher to follow each individual's written language production and comprehension as manifest in the dialogue. Whether the issue at hand is mastery of particular linguistic structures or the grasp of certain ideas in a content-based language class, the writing provides teachers with extensive, ongoing information about where each student stands, and about their strengths and weaknesses as students.

Consider the cases of Sakun and Miguel, two of my beginning ESL students in the same class. Sakun, a Cambodian woman in her thirties, was shy in class. She had had only two years of previous education. Miguel was more outgoing. Not yet twenty, he had completed high school before coming to the United States. Just by watching them, I got a glimpse of their differences. In class, however, both completed the same activities successfully. With almost 30 other students to work with, I simply couldn't keep detailed track of how each was doing or what they needed to work on.

After we began doing dialogue journals, that changed dramatically. Consider the following initial exchanges from their journals, written during class on the same two days:

Sakun

January 26

Dear Paul,

My name is Sakun. i am a student. I am happy. I'm from CAMBoDIA.

Dear Sakun,

Thank you for your beautiful letter. I am from Rhode Island. I know many Cambodian people who live in Providence, Rhode Island. Someday maybe I can visit Cambodia. Sakun, please tell me more about yourself. Are you married? Where do you live?

January 27

*My name is Sakun. I am married. I'm from CAMBODIA.
I have 3 children.*

<u>*Miguel*</u>

January 26

Dear Paul,

*I live in San Francisco. I have one year in this city. I,m
Single, I' like A WOMES, AND I AM 20 years old, I'm like
this school too. Maybe I'm will going to Mexico City, But
no right Now. Maybe two years more, Sincerely, Miguel.*

Dear Miguel,

*Thanks for your letter! I'm happy that you like this school.
Are you from Mexico City? I have been to Mexico City two
times. The last time I went was April, 1987. I loved Mexico
City. It is very big. Please tell me more about yourself.*

January 27

Hi! Paul!

*How are you Today? I'm Think God I'm Happy too, Becose
you like Mexico. Well now I want to tell you somethink
aboutmy life, my father an mother, sisters, and all the
family is in Mexico. I livin in this country for myself., I
have a probns about my work, becose they need that I speak
inglish, These why I coming in this school. I need speak
more inglish, if I want go up, I'm think that everybody need
inglish, but I need right now, becose in two years I'm
working in the same company and then. They say you nee
speak more inglish if you want to make more money. I'm tell
you More about Myself. Sign Miguel. Thanks.*

These brief entries give some sense of the wealth of information the journals can provide. In just a few paragraphs, Miguel demonstrates much greater fluency, a larger vocabulary, and an ability to answer open-ended questions and to elaborate on a topic. In contrast, Sakun struggles to write two lines, answers some but not all of my questions, and repeats herself rather than expand on what she has already said. Miguel's writing also reveals specific needs in spelling, and in the use of prepositions and verb tenses. These brief entries give but a hint of the kind of information I could glean from the journals; over time, I found the writing invaluable in making me aware of how each student was doing with the language, from day to day.

Clearly, dialogue journals can be an important assessment tool. But, they don't stop there. Roger Shuy makes this point, writing about his experience in a graduate seminar on sociolinguistics:

> What was shocking to me...was that the students made clear to me in their journals exactly where they were in their development. This enabled me to individualize my instruction, in their journals, but also in the class itself, in ways I had never done before. Every teacher has general assumptions about the progress of the class as a whole based on clues given by a few. I discovered something that I suppose I should have known; not all students were at the place I thought they were. Some only caught on to the central concepts at the very end. This knowledge, revealed privately in their journals but not made openly in the class, guided me in teaching all 12 of them in different aspects of the course that they needed. I believe I did as much teaching in the journals as I did in the seminar meetings.
>
> (Shuy, 1982, p. 5)

As Shuy's comments suggest, dialogue journals allow teachers to individualize their students' work in two ways. First, teachers can use the information gleaned through journals to tailor individual assignments to particular student needs, either during class or as homework. Perhaps most important, the writing itself can become an important form of individualized instruction.

Teachers can adjust their dialogue journal entries in a variety of ways to their students' individual needs. In interviews with ESL teachers who use dialogue journals, for instance, I have found that many make a point of adjusting the complexity of their writing to what they perceive is each student's linguistic proficiency. To illustrate, a teacher could ask any one of the following questions about essentially the same topic, depending on the student's proficiency:

-Are you married?

-Are you married? What is your wife's name?

-Please tell me about your wife.

-Please tell me about your home life.

Another individualization strategy is to consciously weave specific structures used erroneously by students into individual responses. I do this myself, and have spoken with a number of other teachers who do so consistently.

In their major study of dialogue journal writing with sixth grade ESL students, Joy Kreeft and colleagues (Kreeft et al., 1984) analyzed in detail how one teacher varied diverse aspects of her writing according to differences in her students' language abilities. Jana Staton showed how this teacher varied, more or less systematically, the linguistic complexity and interactive features of her entries according to the students' language proficiency. Joy Kreeft found that the teacher adjusted her questions to each student's language level, and that the complexity of those questions tended to change as the students became more fluent. Roger Shuy documented a complex and probably subconscious but very systematic variation in the teacher's use of language functions according to student use of those same functions. As more research is done with larger samples of teacher-student journal interactions, we hope to learn more about just how individualization in this writing occurs.

Finally, the journals give teachers some welcome flexibility in responding to individual student preferences. I learned how important this can be from Mei Lu, a young Chinese student in my beginning ESL class.

Mei Lu was probably the shyest, most timid student I had ever met.

She wrote very brief entries in her journal, and they were done so lightly in pencil that I often struggled to decipher them. Yet, at the same time, she seemed always to do what was asked of her, including her journal. One day when I took the journals home I noticed with surprise that hers was missing. The next day it reappeared with this entry:

> *I'm sorry I not shoud take the letter at home write, becaaese English letter is difficult and have short time but I hope very sorry*

I responded:

> *You don't need to be sorry. I am happy you took the letter home. I understand you need more time to write. Your letter is very nice. Please take this journal home to write again if you want to.*

Thereafter, Mei Lu often took her journal home, and her writing blossomed; she seemed to write more comfortably and in greater detail about whatever seemed to be on her mind at the time.

ESL instructor Nina Turitz (1982) has described a similar situation with a Taiwanese student who did better when allowed to write at home. As Turitz points out, "A nice advantage to the journal is that a request such as this can be easily fulfilled."

Planning Lessons and Courses

Student entries can give a teacher remarkably consistent and timely feedback on the effectiveness of a particular lesson. The feedback may be indirect, insofar as the students' writing reveals what concepts or linguistic forms they have mastered or are struggling with, or it may be direct, in the form of complaints, questions, or criticisms about a lesson. Either way, this information can be a valuable aid to planning future lessons.

Leslee Reed eloquently sums up her relevant experience with sixth graders:

I find that journal writing is sort of the kernel of my teaching. When I sit down to do journals, I am doing a kind of resume of my day and of each child. As I'm writing each child, I'm mentally thinking about that child. I conjure up in my mind that child on that day....Then as I'm reading his journal I'm seeing if what I sensed as a teacher came through to him as a student. And often it becomes clear that in my lesson plans OK, this did not go over well. I'll need to get this over from a different point of view. So it becomes a planning tool, a core from which I'm planning not only tomorrow's work but, frequently, next week's work. For me, it makes my whole school year flow, because I have a constant finger on the pulse of each student. (Reed, 1988, p. 71)

Although adult ESL students generally write in their journals less often than children and seem to be less likely to give direct feedback on lessons, many of the adult education teachers I have surveyed confirm the usefulness of the journals for planning. A number of teachers have told me that they customarily plan grammar lessons or units around mistakes that recur in a majority of their students' journals. Finding that half of a class consistently forgets question marks and other punctuation, for instance, might prompt a teacher to devote a lesson to those issues. Similarly, in advanced language classes and in courses focused on content, such as American or French culture, student interests and questions, as revealed in the journals, can become the basis for planning particular lessons or activities.

Teaching the Teacher

If ever I am to be a teacher, it will be to learn more than to teach.
Madam Dorothée Deluzy

The greatest rewards of ESL teaching, I've found, come through learning about my students, and through them, about the world. Dialogue journals expand the possibilities for that kind of learning enormously. For me as teacher, they are almost an education in themselves.

Several years ago, one of my ESL classes put together a book of their own compositions. They had been keeping dialogue journals all year, and like their journal writing, the compositions they assembled told of whatever they wanted to write—of families, of love that was strong and of love gone sour, of homes long ago left behind, of losing jobs and of finding new ones, of learning to ski, and of hating to drive. They called it "Pieces of Life."

That's what I think of when I think about my students' journal writing—pieces of life. Reading their entries, I learn far more about them as people, about their cultures, and about the world than would ever be possible otherwise. That is one of dialogue journals' greatest gifts to me as a teacher—they teach me things I could learn in no other way.

Almost any topic is possible in most dialogue journal writing. Teachers might learn about different attitudes and experiences regarding education, religion, family roles, work, play, food, holidays, health, sickness, and even death. In short, human culture in all its diversity can reveal itself in the students' prose. Other teachers I've interviewed have spoken enthusiastically about this benefit of dialogue writing. Leslee Reed captures this feeling when she writes:

> If you ask me what I am getting out of journal writing, particularly in a multi-cultural setting, I'd say it's that I'm learning, I'm learning, I'm learning! Especially with so many cultures, there's such richness. I'm learning every day about little nuances of social behavior and customs and culture. I don't think I've ever grown so much in my life as I have this year in understanding the problems of different cultures, different races, trying to fit into this pattern of American life. I think I have learned to respect other cultures much more.
>
> (Reed, 1988, p. 70)

Sharing cultural tidbits with students can be interesting and fun. The results are not always what one might expect, however. One day, Mei Lu described in detail her family's celebration of Chinese New Year. That night I asked a friend how to write "Happy New Year" in Chinese, which she did for me on a blank scrap of paper. I took it home and diligently copied the characters onto my next entry to Mei Lu.

The next day during our journal writing time I noticed that Mei Lu and her neighbor weren't writing. They seemed to be playing with Mei Lu's journal, turning it around and around. I asked what was going on. Mei Lu turned red and looked down, silently. Her neighbor, an older woman, took me aside and whispered, "You wrote 'Happy New Year' upside down!" As we were all laughing, I thought: Teachers can be slow learners, too!

Growing Through Writing

Dialogue writing helps me to grow both personally and as a writer. In my relationships with others it keeps me alert, for instance, to the countless subtle differences among individuals, differences that I can't appreciate fully during class. It also teaches me about myself, specifically about how I respond to those differences. Being able to read back over previous entries is invaluable in that process. Sometimes, in retrospect, I think that with a given student I've been too abstract, or too personal, or too political. The journals allow me to change my approach in midstream, if need be. They are like a mirror that allows me to look not only at the present, but also at the past.

The practice has also helped me to grow as a writer. Responding to 20 or 30 students day after day stretches my expressive wings, so to speak, in several ways. First, it encourages me to become more versatile with words, and to look for many different sides of the same subject. For example, I often find that a number of students bring up essentially the same topic on any given day, such as families. I may want to respond about that same subject—by discussing my grandfather, for instance—with each student, but without repeating myself exactly in each journal. As a result, I learn to approach a given subject from several different angles.

Second, tailoring my remarks to what I perceive to be subtle differences in different students' interests and language abilities helps to hone my skill at writing to different audiences. As I discussed earlier, this skill is important in many, if not all, written genres, including most formal academic and professional writing, business correspondence, marketing and public relations prose, and even many forms of fiction.

Finally, dialogue journal writing has made personal letter writing easier for me. Before I started doing journals, I rarely corresponded with friends. But, I have found that since I began the practice, writing letters no longer seems so onerous. I enjoy it more, and write with much greater frequency. I now receive many more letters, as well!

Inspiring the Teacher

One of the more intangible but vital benefits to teachers of dialogue writing is that, like few other techniques, dialogue journal writing can help motivate and inspire teachers to teach. I have found this to be true in my own experience, and I've learned that many others share this perception.

Many teachers have told me that doing journals is sometimes the best part of their teaching. This enthusiasm can manifest itself in many ways, some of them a bit surprising. I read one day, for instance, of a teacher in Washington, DC, who was so taken by her students' journals that she couldn't wait to get home to read them. She would flip through them while driving home on the expressway. (Melody Schneider, elsewhere in this volume, describes opening her students' journals at the subway stop on her way home.) I chuckled when I read this because I, too, have done the same thing more than once.

Beyond being compelling, the interaction can be deeply rewarding. For me, the connection to the students as people is so powerful, the feeling so gratifying, that it can give whole new meaning to my daily work in teaching. It renews a sense of value in my classroom work and strengthens my knowledge that I am there both to grow myself and to participate in the growth of others.

The day in class can seem difficult, and lesson planning endless, but when I sit down to do the journals, little else matters. It is sometimes the best part of my teaching. And I know from talking with other teachers that I am not alone in this feeling.

References

Bruner, J. (1988). Foreword to *Dialogue journal communication: Classroom, linguistic, social and cognitive views*. In J. Staton, R.W. Shuy, J.K. Peyton, & L. Reed. Norwood, NJ: Ablex.

Burling, R. (1982). *Sounding right: An introduction to comprehension-based language instruction*. Rowley, MA: Newbury House.

Curran, C. (1976). *Counseling learning in second languages*. Apple River, IL: Apple River Press.

Fillmore, C. (1979). On fluency. In C. Fillmore et al, (Eds.), *Individual differences in language ability and language behavior* (pp. 85-101). New York: Academic Press.

Gutstein, S.P. (1987). *Toward the assessment of communicative competence writing: An analysis of the dialogue journal writing of Japanese adult ESL students*. Unpublished doctoral dissertation, Georgetown University, Washington, DC.

Krashen, S.D. (1982). *Principles and practice in second language acquisition*. Oxford: Pergamon Press.

Kreeft, J. (1984). Dialogue writing—Bridge from talk to essay writing. *Language Arts, 61*, 141-150.

Kreeft, J., Shuy, R.W., Staton, J., Reed, L., & Morroy, R. (1984). *Dialogue writing: Analysis of student-teacher interactive writing in the learning of English as a second language* (NIE-G-83-0030). Washington, DC: Center for Applied Linguistics. (ERIC Document Reproduction Service No. ED 252 097)

Long, M.H. (1983). Native speaker/nonnative speaker conversation and the negotiation of comprehensible input. *Applied Linguistics, 4*, 126-141.

Peyton, J.K., & Reed, L. (1990). *Dialogue journal writing with nonnative English speakers: A handbook for teachers*. Washington, DC: Teachers of English to Speakers of Other Languages.

Peyton, J.K., Staton, J., Richardson G., & Wolfram, W. (1990). The influence of writing task on ESL students' written production. *Research in the Teaching of English, 24*(2), 142-171.

Reed, L. (1988). Dialogue journals make my whole year flow: The teacher's perspective. In J. Staton, R.W. Shuy, J.K. Peyton, & L. Reed. *Dialogue journal communication: Classroom, linguistic, social and cognitive views* (pp. 56-72). Norwood, NJ: Ablex.

Shuy, R.W. (1980). *Developing writing dialogue out of speech dialogue.* Paper presented at the National Council of Teachers of English, San Antonio, Texas.

Shuy, R.W. (1982). Some applications of DJ's—college/graduate school. *Dialogue, (1),* 5.

Shuy, R.W. (1988). Sentence level language functions. In J. Staton, R.W. Shuy, J.K. Peyton, & L. Reed, *Dialogue journal communication: Classroom, linguistic, social and cognitive views* (pp. 107-142). Norwood, NJ: Ablex.

Staton, J. (in press). Language input and interaction: Developing a written conversation. In J.K. Peyton & J. Staton, *Dialogue journals in the multilingual classroom: Building language fluency and writing skills through written interaction.* Norwood, NJ: Ablex.

Staton, J. (1986). The teacher's writing as text. *GreaterWashington Reading Council Journal, 11,* 3-4.

Staton, J. (1985). Using dialogue journals for developing thinking, reading, and writing with hearing impaired students. *The Volta Review, 7,* 127-154.

Staton, J., Peyton, J.K., & Gutstein, S. (Eds.), (1988). Dialogue journals in international settings. *Dialogue, 5,* 1-19.

Turitz, N. (1982). Dialogue journals in adult ESL programs. *Dialogue,* 1(2), 5-6.

Vanett, L., & Jurich, D. (1990). The missing link: Connecting journal writing to academic writing. In J.K. Peyton (Ed.), *Students and teachers writing together: Perspectives on journal writing* (pp. 21-33). Washington, DC: Teachers of English to Speakers of Other Languages.

Dialogue Journal Resources

There is extensive material available for the teacher who desires to know more about dialogue journal use and research with many different student populations, but very little material focusing specifically on nonnative English speaking adults developing their literacy abilities—the reason this book is so important. Articles in one issue of the newsletter *Dialogue* focus on this population:

> Dialogue journals for developing literacy in refugee,
> migrant, and adult basic education. *Dialogue*, 3(3),
> September, 1986.

Apart from that, publications about dialogue journal writing with *adults* learning English as a second language have to do with deaf and hearing adults in colleges. All of these articles provide useful information for working with other adult ESL population

Journal Writing with Adults

Hearing ESL College Students
Gutstein, S.P. (1983). Using language functions to measure fluency. [EDRS No. ED 240 871]

Meloni, C. F. (1983). What do university ESL students write about in dialogue journals? [EDRS No. ED 240 885]

Spack, R., & Sadow, C. (1983). Student-teacher working journals in ESL freshman composition. *TESOL Quarterly, 17*(4), 575-593. [EJ 291 770]

Steer, J. Dialogue journal writing for academic purposes. [EDRS No. 295 479]

Steffensen, M. S. (1988). The dialogue journal: A method for improving cross-cultural reading comprehension. *Reading in a Foreign Language, 5*(1), 193-203. [EJ 388 983]

Deaf and Hard of Hearing College Students

Many deaf and hard of hearing adults have limited proficiency with written English because they have limited access to oral English. In many cases, written English is a second language for them. Therefore, articles and handbooks written for teachers working with this population are particularly useful for those working with hearing adult literacy learners who are nonnative English speakers.

Albertini, J. (1990). Coherence in deaf students' writing. In J. K. Peyton (Ed.), *Students and teachers writing together: Perspectives on journal writing* (pp. 127-136). Washington, DC: TESOL.

Albertini, J., & Meath-Lang, B. (1986). Analysis of student-teacher exchanges in dialogue journal writing. *Journal of Curriculum Theorizing, 7*, 1-14.

Cannon, B., & Polio, C. (1989). An analysis of input and interaction in the dialogue journals of deaf community college students. *Teaching English to Deaf and Second Language Students, 7*(1), 12-21.

Meath-Lang, B. (1990). The dialogue journal: Reconceiving curriculum and teaching. In J. K. Peyton (Ed.), *Students and teachers writing together: Perspectives on journal writing* (pp. 5-17). Washington, DC: TESOL.

Staton, J. (Ed.). *Conversations in writing: A guide to using dialogue journals with deaf post-secondary and secondary students.* Available from Gallaudet Research Institute, Gallaudet University, 800 Florida Ave., NW, Washington, DC 20002.

Walworth, M. (1990). Interactive teaching of reading: A model. In J. K. Peyton (Ed.), *Students and teachers writing together: Perspectives on journal writing* (pp. 37-47). Washington, DC: TESOL. [See also, "Dialogue journals and the teaching of reading," EJ 320 020, for a similar version of the article.]

Preservice and In-service Teacher Training

Since staff in adult literacy programs are beginning to use dialogue journals in literacy teacher and tutor training (as described in several articles in this volume), publications focusing on dialogue journal use with prospective and experienced teachers of other student populations are useful as well.

Bishop, W. (1989). Teachers as learners: Negotiated roles in college writing teachers' learning logs. [EDRS No. ED 304 690]

Brinton, D., & Holten, C. (1989). What novice teachers focus on: The practicum in TESL. *TESOL Quarterly, 23* (2), 343-350. [EJ 393 799]

Fishman, A. R., & Rover, E. J. (1989). "Maybe I'm just *not* teacher material:" Dialogue journals in the student teaching experience. *English Education, 21*(2), 92-109. [EJ 388 572]

Flores, B., & García, E. A. (1984). A collaborative learning and teaching experience using dialogue journal writing. *NABE Journal, 8*(2), 67-83. [EJ 307 294]

Roderick, J. (1986). Dialogue writing: Context for reflecting on self as teacher and researcher. *Journal of Curriculum and Supervision, 1*(4), 305-315. [EJ 338 767]

Roderick, J., & Berman, L. (1984). Dialoguing about dialogue journals: Teachers as learners. *Language Arts, 61*(7), 686-692. [EJ 306 641]

Staton, J., Peyton, J. K., & Gutstein, S. (Eds.). (September, 1988). Interactive writing in teacher education [Theme issue]. *Dialogue, 5*(2).

For those wishing to conduct teacher training workshops, a workshop packet is also available. It includes detailed guidelines for conducting the workshop, over 30 samples of student writing that can be made into overhead transparencies, background materials for the presenter, and handouts. The packet is available from the Center for Applied Linguistics, 1118 22nd Street NW, Washington, DC 20037, attention: *Dialogue*.

131

Dialogue Journal Writing with Other Student Populations

Publications about dialogue journal use with other student populations still have helpful information for work with adults. Articles, books, and handbooks are listed here by topic focus:

General Articles, Useful with Any Population

Kreeft, J. (1984). Dialogue journal writing: Bridge from talk to essay writing. *Language Arts, 61*(2), 141-150. [EJ 293 064]

Lindfors, J. (1988). From "talking together" to "being together in talk." *Language Arts, 61*(2), 135-141. [EJ 367 218]

Sayers, D. (1986, December). "Interactive" writing with computers: One solution to the time problem. *Dialogue, 3*(4), 9-10.

Shuy, R. W. (1984, Summer). Language as a foundation for education in the school context. *Theory into Practice,* 167-174.

Shuy, R. W. (1987). Research currents: Dialogue as the heart of learning. *Language Arts, 64*(8), 890-897. [EJ 357 929]

Staton, J. (1983, March). Dialogue journals: A new tool for teaching communication. *ERIC/CLL News Bulletin, 6*(2), pp. 1-6.

Staton, J. (1987). The power of responding in dialogue journals. In T. Fulwiler (Ed.), *The journal book.* Portsmouth, NH: Boynton/Cook.

Staton, J. (1988). ERIC/RCS report: Dialogue journals. *Language Arts, 65*(2), 198-201. [EJ 267 224]

Staton, J., & Shuy, R. W. (1988). Talking our way into writing and reading: Dialogue journal practice. In B. A. Raforth & D. L. Rubin (Eds.), *The social construction of written communication* (pp. 195-217). Norwood, NJ: Ablex.

Staton, J., Shuy, R. W., Peyton, J. K., & Reed, L. (1988). *Dialogue journal communication: Classroom, linguistic, social and cognitive views.* Norwood, NJ: Ablex.

With Nonnative English Speaking Students

Lindfors, J. W. (1988). From helping hand to reciprocity to mutuality: Dialogue journal writing with Zulu students. *Journal of Learning, 1*(1), 83-85.

Lindfors, J. W. (1988). Zulu students' questioning in dialogue journals. *Questioning Exchange, 2*(3), 289-304.

Peyton, J. K. (1986, Fall). Interactive writing: Making writing meaningful for language minority students. *NABE News,* 19-21.

Peyton, J. K. (1989). Dialogue journal writing and the acquisition of English grammatical morphology. In J. K. Peyton (Ed.), *Students and teachers writing together: Perspectives on journal writing.* (pp. 67-97). Washington, DC: TESOL.

Peyton, J. K., & Seyoum, M. (1989). The effect of teacher strategies on ESL students' interactive writing: The case of dialogue journals. *Research in the Teaching of English,* 23 (3), 310-334. [EJ 396 487]

Peyton, J. K., & Staton, J. (in press). *Dialogue journals in the multilingual classroom: Building language fluency and writing skills through written interaction.* Norwood, NJ: Ablex.

Sayers, D. (1986). Sending messages: Across the classroom and around the world. *TESOL Newsletter* [Supplement on computer-assisted language learning], *20*(1), 7-8.

Staton, J., Peyton, J. K., & Gutstein, S. (Eds.). (1986, March). Dialogue journals in ESL settings [Theme issue]. *Dialogue, 3*(2).

Staton, J., Peyton, J. K., & Gutstein, S. (Eds.). (1988, December). Interactive writing in bilingual education [Theme issue]. *Dialogue, 5*(3).

With Migrant Students

Davis, F. (1983). Why you call me emigrant?: Dialogue journal writing with migrant youth. *Childhood Education, 60*(2), 110-116. [EJ 288 593]

Hayes, C. W., & Bahruth, R. (1985). Querer es poder. In J. Hansen, T. Newkirk & D. Graves (Eds.), *Breaking ground: Teachers relate reading and writing in the elementary school* (pp. 97-108). Portsmouth, NH: Heinemann.

With Native Americans

Dooley, M. S. (1987). *Dialogue journals: Facilitating the reading-writing connection with native American students.* [EDRS No. ED 292 118]

With Young Children

Bailes, C., Searles, S., Slobodzian, J., & Staton, J. (1986). *It's your turn now: A handbook for teachers of deaf students.* Available from Outreach

PreCollege Program, KDES, PAS 6, 800 Florida Avenue NE, Washington, DC 20002, (202) 651-5031.

Bode, B. A. (1989). Dialogue journal writing. *Reading Teacher*, 42(8), 568-571.

Braig, D. (1986). Six authors in search of an audience. In B. Schiefflen (Ed.), *The acquisition of literacy: Ethnographic perspectives* (pp. 110-113). Norwood, NJ: Ablex.

Britton, J. (1987). *Reading and writing in the classroom*. Berkeley, CA: Center for the Study of Writing.

Farley, J. W., & Farley, S. L. (1987). Interactive writing and gifted children: Communication through literacy. *Journal for the Education of the Gifted*, 10(2), 99-106. [EJ 352 440]

Flores, B., & García, E. (1984). A collaborative learning and teaching experience using journals. *NABE Journal*, 8, 67-83. [EJ 307 294]

Hall, N. (Ed.). (1989). *Writing with reason: The emergence of authorship in young children* (selected chapters). Portsmouth, NH: Heinemann.

Hall, N., & Duffy, R. (1987). Every child has a story to tell. *Language Arts*, 64(5), 523-529. [EJ 357 928]

Kitagawa, M., & Kitagawa, C. (1987). Journal writing. In M. Kitagawa & C. Kitagawa (Eds.), *Making connections with writing: An expressive writing model in Japanese schools* (pp. 58-66). Portsmouth, NH: Heinemann.

Peyton, J. K. (1990). Beginning at the beginning. In A.M. Padilla, H. H. Fairchild, & C. M. Valadez (Eds.), *Bilingual education: Issues and strategies* (pp. 195-218). Newbury Park, CA: Sage Publications.

Staton, J. (1984). Thinking together: Interaction in children's reasoning. In C. Thaiss & C. Suhor (Eds.), *Speaking and writing, K-12* (pp. 144-187). Champaign, IL: National Council of Teachers of English.

Staton, J. (1985). Using dialogue journals for developing thinking, reading, and writing with hearing-impaired students. *Volta Review*, 7(5), 127-154.

Staton, J., Peyton, J. K., Gutstein, S. (Eds.). (April, 1989). Interactive writing in elementary education [Theme issue]. *Dialogue*, 6(1).

With Special Needs Students

Farley, J. W. (1986). Analysis of written dialogue of educable mentally retarded writers. *Education and Training of the Mentally Retarded, 21*(3), 181-191.

Farley, J. W., & Farley, S. L. (1987). Interactive writing and gifted children: Communication through literacy. *Journal for the Education of the Gifted, 10*(2), 99-106. [EJ 352 440]

Flores, B., Rueda, F., & Porter, B. (1986). Examining assumptions and instructional practices related to the acquisition of literacy with bilingual special education students. In A. C. Willig & H. F. Greenberg (Eds.), *Bilingualism and learning disabilities: Policy and practice for teachers and administrators.* New York: American Library Publishing.

Goldman, S., & Rueda, R. (1988). Developing writing skills in bilingual exceptional children. *Exceptional Children, 54*(6), 543-551. [EJ 368 919]

McGettigan, K. (1987). Dialogue journals: An initiation into writing. *Journal of Reading, Writing and Learning Disabilities International, 3*(4), 321-326. [EJ 375 001]

Staton, J., Peyton, J. K., & Gutstein, S. (Eds.). (May, 1985). Dialogue journals with students with special needs [Theme issue]. *Dialogue, 2*(4).

Staton, J., & Tyler, D. (1987). Dialogue journal use with learning-disabled students. *Pointer, 32*(1), 4-8. [EJ 363 520]

Dialogue Journals and Writing

Farr, M., & Janda, M. A. (1985). Basic writing students: Investigating oral and written language. *Research in the Teaching of English, 19*(1), 62-83. [EJ 309 865]

Kreeft, J. (1984). Dialogue writing: Bridge from talk to essay writing. *Language Arts, 61*(2), 141-150. [EJ 293 064]

McGuire, B. (1986). Where does the teacher intervene with under-achieving writers? [EDRS No. ED 285 193]

Peyton, J. K. (1986). Literacy through written interaction. *Passage: A Journal for Refugee Education, 2*(1), 24-29. [EDRS No. ED 273 097]

Peyton, J. K., Staton, J., Richardson, G., & Wolfram, W.(1990). The influence of writing task on ESL students' written production. *Research in the Teaching of English, 24*(2), 142-171.

Staton, J. (1981, October). Literacy as an interactive process. *The Linguistic Reporter,* pp. 1-5.

Dialogue Journals and Reading

Atwell, N. (1977). *In the middle: Writing, reading and learning with adolescents.* Upper Montclair, NJ: Boynton/Cook.

Atwell, N. (1984). Writing and reading literature from the inside out. *Language Arts, 61*(3), 240-252. [EJ 294 796]

Gambrell, L. B. (1985). Dialogue journals: Reading-writing interaction. *The Reading Teacher, 38*(6), pp. 512-515. [EJ 311 558]

Staton, J. (1986). The teacher's writing as text. *Greater Washington Reading Council Journal, 11,* 3-4.

Steffensen, M. S. (1988). The dialogue journal: A method for improving cross-cultural reading comprehension. *Reading in a Foreign Language, 5*(1), 193-203. [EJ 388 983]

Walworth, M. (1990). Interactive teaching of reading: A model. In J. K. Peyton (Ed.), *Students and teachers writing together: Perspectives on journal writing* (pp. 37-47), Washington, DC: TESOL.

Dialogue Journals and Content Instruction

Borasi, R., & Rose, B. J. (1989). Journal writing and mathematics instruction. *Educational Studies in Mathematics, 20*(4), 347-365. [EJ 406 045]

Rose, B. J. (1989). Writing and mathematics: Theory and practice. In P. Connolly and T. Vilardi (Eds.), *Writing to learn mathematics and science.* NY: Teachers College Press.

Staton, J., Peyton, J. K., & Gutstein, S. (Eds.). (September, 1989). Interactive writing in content-area instruction. [Theme issue]. *Dialogue, 6*(2).

Note

This resource list has been adapted and extended, with permission, from a list published in *Dialogue journal writing with nonnative English speaking students: A handbook for teachers* by J.K. Peyton and L. Reed, 1990, available from TESOL, 1600 Cameron Street, Suite 300, Alexandria, VA 22314. Items with ED numbers are available from the ERIC Document Reproduction Service (EDRS), 3900 Wheeler Avenue, Alexandria, VA 22304, 1-800-227-3742. Items with EJ numbers can be located in the journal cited in the reference, or they can be ordered from University Microfilms International (UMI) Article Clearinghouse, 300 North Zeeb Road, Ann Arbor, MI 48106, 800-732-0616.